NO BLADE OF GRASS...

NO BLADE OF GRASS...

**HECTOR
CHRISTIE**

First published in 1997 by Christie Publishing, Tapeley Park, Instow, North Devon, EX39 4NT, United Kingdom

The right of Hector Christie to be identified as author of this work has been asserted in accordance with the Copyright, Designs and Patents Act 1988

ISBN 0 9530459 0 0

Printed and bound by Creative Print & Design (Wales), Ebbw Vale

DEDICATION

This book is dedicated to Kirsty.

ABOUT THE AUTHOR

Hector Christie was born in 1961 at Glyndebourne (his family own and run Glyndebourne Opera House) and educated at Eton, spending his school holidays on a local farm learning the care of sheep, cattle and turkeys. Following training at Sealle-Hayne Agricultural College and work in Australia and Zambia he settled in North Devon to farm, where he divided his time between farming, surfing and playing football. In March 1988, following the death of his aunt, he took over the running of Tapeley Park and Gardens, a stately home with nationally renowned Italianate gardens owned by the Christie family which is open to the public throughout the summer. Hector's spiritual and ecological studies have resulted in a large exhibition permaculture garden also being established at Tapeley. This he fits in whilst playing enthusiastically for Torrington Football Club in the Western League.

ACKNOWLEDGEMENTS

My love and sincere thanks to:-

Harry Sadi and Tina Roberts for their down to earth, objective appraisal and criticism in helping me write this book. Also, to my brother Toll for his painstakingly thorough proof-reading.

And finally, a thank you to Debra Affleck, for her assistance in preparing this manuscript.

Contents

PREFACE

I am convinced everybody should have the freedom to believe in whatever they choose, if anything at all. There are many, many different paths to the *same goal*, and any one individual or doctrine, sect or cult should *never push* their beliefs on anyone else.

This piece is based on my personal 'experiences' and for those who read it I would ask you to question and be sceptical, yet broad minded and objective as I believe we should be whatever religious teachings, stories or rumours reach our ears.

One of my objectives in writing this book is that anybody can read it and get something out of it - hence the chapter on Definitions stating what I mean by Karma, the Ethereal Realm/ Body and so on at the beginning of this book. If the reader is new to the subject, then all the points are unlikely to be fully understood at the first read. Therefore, it will help to read this book slowly and ruminate on the points that draw your attention, then put it on the top shelf and have the odd look at it again in the future - if you feel like it!

Whether you agree with my 'conviction' of the Levels, God, Lucifer etc., is not important or the point. This book illustrates how I perceive the Truth, so to be objective means simply to focus on the underlying principles and not to get stuck on one or more points you may feel to be a load of rubbish, thereby clouding the rest of it and making any further reading a waste of time. This same principle applies whether you think Christ, for example, was the Son of God, a Prophet or simply a very enlightened person.

I've tried to write this book stressing what I believe is important and what isn't. Splitting hairs over details often serves no other purpose than to confuse us through over complication, which then more often than not, results in our losing interest. I'm a great believer in the simplicity of the Universe and the way it operates. The greatest inventions on earth are generally so simple we don't see them even when they're staring us in the face, and the same goes for 'supposed' Spiritual mysteries.

We all have a responsibility to the collective group and the planet every day of our lives. However, I believe that within this framework we are here on earth to learn our *OWN* individual lessons and have to find out what they are on *our own*. To blindly believe another's doctrine, is to take the easy way and is of little benefit to our Spiritual Growth. When a disaster or tragedy happens which turns our lives upside down, how often have we heard it said:- 'How could God do this to me or my mother, brother, friend etc.' The implication of this kind of remark is that God is some man in the sky, albeit more 'advanced' than us, who is himself directly pulling all the strings and maybe makes the odd mistake. For example, if He has got a lot on his plate one day, He may not notice a couple of terrorists planting a bomb in their husband's or wife's office block. If this book helps open the door slightly for just one person and for them to start questioning the 'whys' and 'wherefores', it will have been worth it.

The main problem that I've found in writing this book has been that because most of the chapters are so interrelated, it has been very difficult to deal with each topic independent of the others. For example, regarding the chapters on Fear and

Faith, it is impossible to deal with one without discussing the other. The same applies when taking the chapters on Judgement, Humility and Self-Righteousness. This is why I refer a lot to other chapters, to save long winded repetitions of previous points.

> Our highest truths are but half-truths;
> Think not to settle down for ever in any truth.
> Make use of it as a tent in which to pass a summer's night,
> But build no house of it, or it will be your tomb.
> When you first have an inkling of its insufficiency
> And begin to descry a dim counter-truth looming up beyond,
> Then weep not, but give thanks:
> It is the Lord's voice whispering,
> 'Take up thy bed and walk'.
> Passage from Earl Balfour.

This book only just scratches the surface and is simply intended to invite thought, not preach yet another form of dogma.

INTRODUCTION

'No Blade of Grass is blown without Divine Intention' - this includes the Blade of Grass itself. God in His 'Omnipresence, Omnipotence and Omniscience', understands the needs of every living cell in the Universe. His Will determines the time taken for the grass seed to germinate, relative to ground temperature; its speed of growth, health and vigour, relative to the amount of wind, sunlight, and rainfall absorbed by the roots; and its time and cause of death, whether it be given up to the benefit of life's process for a grazing animal, or whether it dies by natural senescence in the cold of winter, having 'given of itself' by helping to maintain the atmosphere through photosynthesis. In God's eyes blades of grass are just as significant as the Holiest of men, since everyone and everything is connected within the ever-moving wheel of God's Perfect Creation. 'But the very hairs on your head are all numbered.' Matthew 10 vs 30.

No Blade of Grass ..... How often have many of us run into friends or acquaintances when in some far off country, and heard people say 'what a small world!' The Divine Intention may be just to give us a boost when we're lonely, or if we'd always thought the person was a complete so and so, and ended up having to sit next to them on a bus across Africa, we'd be forced, for our own sanity to search for the good points in that individual, making us possibly a more loving person.

When standing in a long check-out queue, an 'Enlightened'

person is in a state of *grace* - 'God centredness' - and smiles, knowing 'No Blade of Grass ...,' in that *wherever we are and whatever we are doing is perfect for our spirit at that moment*, giving us the opportunities to grow or sink. Hence, everything happens for a purpose to assist our Spirit to grow (God's omniscience/all-knowing). For example, if we lose our cool in the check-out queue, then clearly we have the lesson of patience to work on; or maybe we're being held up to coincide with bumping into someone in the car park or bus station that 'we need to see'.

There's *no such thing as coincidence.* This means nothing happens by chance, is bad luck and there are no accidents. Consequently we can feel sometimes like a puppet on a string. However, we should remember that it is the interaction of our Free Will together with the Will of God, that pulls those strings. This being the case, if we expand this concept throughout the whole of History from the beginning of time, we find that our ancestry, past lives, our parents, brothers, sisters and so on are all perfect for our Spiritual lessons AND we for theirs. 'The whole Universe is my University, I am the only student and everyone and everything are my professors.'

A NUMEROLOGY EXERCISE - demonstrating No Blade of Grass .... is if we take the total number of Chapters in the bible - 1189 and isolate 1 (the middle one), it leaves 1188 - divide by 2 leaves 594 Chapters either side of the one in the middle. 'Coincidentally' the Chapter in the middle is Psalm 118, and taking verse 8 to give the number 1188, it states:- 'It is better to trust in the Lord than to put confidence in man' - what more do we need to know? 'Coincidentally' as well, Psalm 118 lies between the shortest Chapter, Psalm 117, and the longest Chapter, Psalm 119.

1. DEFINITIONS

EVOLUTION

In order for there to be Creation, something must have created it. This 'something' is referred to by a huge variety of names the world over: God, Jah, Allah, Krishna, The Source, The Creator and many more. However, in this text, It, He, and She will be referred to as God. Creation must have Order, Structure and Purpose, and it is through His Will that this is maintained via the ever moving cycle of change and hopefully progress (which is down to each one of us individually and collectively).

Hence, in the Beginning, God put into effect His Will summarised below for the purpose of this text as the *four laws of creation/nature*, out of which all subsequent Laws can be said to be derived:

THE FOUR LAWS:

1. THE LAW OF RETURNS or Reciprocal Action - We reap whatever we sow, re. Cause and Effect - good or bad - *our responsibility*. This is the LAW OF KARMA. All Karma must and will return. For example, if in a past life we sowed a seed that was not good and nothing was done, we may be born a cripple, for example, or become crippled by an accident through which the past Karma is cleared and resolved. The extent and exact nature of our *karmic debt* corresponds to the

past seed sown, of which we are naturally unaware in this lifetime. However, by truly and sincerely exerting ourselves to do good deeds, think good thoughts, control our mouths and 'love thy neighbour as thyself', we can greatly modify the nature and result of the returning Karmic repercussions.

2. THE LAW OF ATTRACTION or Like Attracts Like - All things of a like nature, both seen and unseen, are attracted: For example, an angry person attracts or is attracted to angry people/situations. Likewise, if we have a fault in our make up, *our nature* will attract or be drawn to people and situations which bring this particular emotion to our attention: *our responsibility*.

3. THE LAW OF GRAVITATION - The more aligned we are to God's Will, the 'lighter' we become and the more we rise to God, now, and at death when we gravitate to the level of our corresponding 'Inner Density'. The reverse being the case, the more we succumb to temptations - *our responsibility*. 'Inner Density' refers to the state of our Spirit, i.e. the extent to which our spirit is heavy, clouded and contaminated as opposed to light, pure and aligned with the Will of God.

4. THE LAW OF EQUILIBRIUM - It is our collective vibrations of hatred or love, fear or faith, which create our surroundings and the world we live in. Energy in the form of thought, action and word, cannot be destroyed (basic physics), and in an overall sense, the greater mass overcomes the lesser - again our individual and collective *responsibility*.

All these Four Laws are inseparable and interwoven. They could be simplified and indeed are all contained in the adage:- 'For whatsoever a man soweth, that shall he also reap,' Galatians 6 vs 7. For example, the 'Karmic' challenges, opportunities and 'apparent' coincidences that we 'attract', solely depend on how we have coped with the same up until then; the state of our Inner Density reflects all our past activities; and collectively these directly affect our surroundings. The Parable of the sower suggests that we reap what we sow many times over:- 'But he that received seed into the good ground is he that heareth the word, and understandeth it: which also beareth fruit, and bringeth forth, some one hundred fold, some sixty, some thirty.' Matthew 13 vs 23.

All religions contain the principle of cause and effect. However, this law has been divided into many subdivisions to give examples of it operating in a variety of ways. Truth and Justice - God's Will, is *very simple* - an acorn grows into an oak tree producing many thousands of acorns - we can either sow love or hatred, good or evil; which would you rather sow?

REINCARNATION: The Physical Body we have is temporary and our Spirit is eternal (this concept is described in detail in the 'Human Being' definition). Hence, when our body dies, our Spirit lives on returning periodically to operate in another body for more 'Karmic' lessons, which gives our Spirit further opportunities to grow towards the Light. This process of reincarnation will continue indefinitely until we have paid off all our Karmic debts and no longer succumb to any temptations. It is only then that we will truly enter Heaven and break free from this Karmic cycle forever. The time taken to achieve eternal peace depends upon the efforts of each individual - our responsibility.

'GOOD' AND 'EVIL': Multiple theories abound as to the definition of 'Good' and 'Evil', but fortunately the vast majority contain the same underlying principles. God stands for all things Good, as the name suggests, and His Will is described in more detail in the Chapter on God's Will. Many feel Lucifer, often referred to as the Ruler of Darkness and Evil, is a fallen Angel whose objective is to defile the whole of God's Creation. But, as in many such things unseen on such vast Universal issues, exact details are not important and often distracting.

However, what is important and clear is that God in his love for mankind gave us 'Free Will'. In other words, we are all ultimately responsible for our actions. 'But if ye have bitter envying and strife in your hearts, glory not, and lie not against the truth. This wisdom descendeth not from above, but is earthly, sensual, devilish. For where envying and strife is, there is confusion and every evil work. But the wisdom that is from above is first pure, then peaceable, gentle, and easy to be intreated, full of mercy and good fruits, without partiality, and without hypocrisy. And the fruit of righteousness is sown in peace of them that make peace.' James 3 vs 14 - 18. Our base emotions or those of love determine whether we gravitate towards Heaven (the Light) or hell. To move towards the light, we need to project unconditional love to all mankind and demonstrate humility in all situations. On the other hand, if we succumb to the temptations which we face daily, such as blaming others for *anything* whether we be 'right' or 'wrong', we will gravitate towards hell (darkness). This concept is developed throughout this book. I believe that energy is a neutral force, and it's up to us how we use it, either for good or ill, with all the corresponding ramifications for our Spirit at every turn (detailed in Chapter on Lucifer).

In this book, when I refer to Lucifer, I don't mean a multi-headed, fork tailed, fire breathing monster, but simply The Universal Energy being used for the purpose of evil and/or anything that results in our Spirit increasing in density and moving away from the Light. Therefore, whenever I mention

Lucifer in the text, I am referring to the Lucifer *energy*. The like attracts like principle is very apparent when 'Satanists' try to 'summon up the Devil'. The nastier the person or group doing the rituals, the nastier the Energy or Entities that are attracted. This same principle naturally applies to those gravitating towards the Light.

'Where your attention goes your energy flows.' This not only applies to the choice of whether we wish to bring light or darkness into our lives, but also if we are fearful or even paranoid of 'dark forces', we will attract these energies even if our fundamental volition is for good. The power of our thought should never be underestimated.

CREATION

'THE SPIRITUAL REALM', or True Heaven should be everyone's target, but we can only enter when totally pure in thought, word and deed and once we have paid all our Karmic debts. The light here is too bright for Lucifer or any darkness. This is where we originated from as immature Spirit Sparks, to pass through all the necessary Karmic experiences, so that we can return as a mature Spirit. A microcosm of this is life on earth, where an innocent baby grows, learns and develops, then dies as a mature adult (hopefully), taking the experiences/ lessons with them onto the next stage.

'First be reconciled to thy brother and then come and offer thy gift. Agree with thine adversary quickly whiles thou art in the way with him: lest at any time the adversary deliver thee to the judge, and the judge deliver thee to the officer, and thou be cast into prison. Verily I say unto thee, Thou shalt by no means come out thence, until thou hast paid the uttermost farthing.' Matthew 5 vs 24 - 26. The quicker we can settle our every score and boldly tackle everything that is thrown at us, with *love, humility* and *forgiveness*, the sooner we can leave prison - the Karmic Realms, and enter Heaven: But, this can only happen when we have paid the 'uttermost farthing' of our Karmic debt. Hence, nothing is a waste of time and every moment is precious, but to get 'Home' may take many lifetimes over many millennia. This is solely down to *US* individually, growing or sinking according to our every action, thought and word in conjunction with God's Universal Laws (discussed in Chapter on God's Will).

THE ETHERIC - After the physical death of our body, we pass into the Etheric Realm. Here the physical vessel for our

Spirit is gone, which combined with the fact that we are *compartmentalised* according to our Inner Density, means that our Spirit is exposed to and mingles with only those of 'like' entities around us. Hence, there could be thousands upon thousands of levels in this Realm. This concept is expanded upon in The Overview at the end of this chapter. Indeed, there are many levels of hell, as there are of higher levels and those in between, with the presence and influence of darkness decreasing the lighter the level to which the individual's Spirit gravitates. 'In my Father's house are many mansions.' John 14 vs 2.

THE HIGH AND MID ETHERIC: The higher the level to which we gravitate, the more we will realise that we create our own surroundings. The power of our thought 'seems' to escalate the lighter we are. For example, should we desire to live in a beautiful garden or on a lovely beach we create our surroundings by our thoughts in alignment with God's Will (discussed later). These thoughts tend to overlap with others of a like mind (c.f. some peoples memories of their near death experiences). Likewise, as we move towards the Lower Etheric, where Spirits are holding on to thoughts such as hatred, anger, bitterness and sorrow, we again create our own ethereal surroundings, reflecting that which we feel we deserve - again overlapping with others of a like mind.

THE LOWER ETHERIC - is the darkest of all the realms. This is where we end up after our own individual time of judgement at our physical death if we have led a 'bad' or 'evil' life or just stubbornly refused to learn from the lessons and opportunities 'given' to us. 'A good tree cannot bring forth evil fruit, neither can a corrupt tree bring forth good fruit.' Matthew 7 vs 18. Throughout our many individual days of judgement which occur at the end of each of our earthly lives, as distinct from the Global Judgement Day for the whole of mankind (discussed in Chapter on God's Will), we are simply shown ourselves to ourselves by the 'light of God' - the Four Laws. If we have not brought forth 'good fruit', then the shame felt by our Spirit could be so great that it flees as far as it can into the darkness of the Lower Etheric to hide from the harsh reality of being 'exposed' in every conceivable way in the light.

'Whatsoever ye shall bind on earth shall be bound in heaven: and whatsoever ye shall loose on earth shall be loosed in heaven.' Matthew 18 vs 18. As in all things, the answers lie in tackling our emotions, in that the more we hold on to our base emotions, such as anger, resentment, jealousy, intense fear, guilt and so on and our base desires (carnal, material and social), the harder it will be for us to face the light/ourselves.

Because there is no change in our psyche at death (see footnote for 'mitigating circumstances'), i.e. we are still the same person afterwards mentally, emotionally and in our hearts, then by holding on to things of the earth whilst alive we will continue to hold on to the same things when we die. This is why many such Spirits are called *earthbound spirits*, because they can't let go of their material possessions, contemporaries, status, emotions and so on and therefore remain 'bound' to the earth. It is because of the density (i.e. lack of 'lightness') of these Spirits, which makes them remain 'part' physical, and means that some can move and sometimes hurl things round a room. Such Spirits are often called Poltergeists and they tend to have experienced some sort of major trauma when they were alive, such as suicide, intense suffering, murder and so on, of which they cannot let go. The significance of the moving of objects is discussed in the Chapter on Lucifer and a description of life in the Lower Etheric is given in the Footnote in the same Chapter. Not all Earthbound Spirits are poltergeists. There are many gentler, yet still emotionally traumatised Spirits who may be bound by family or house/home and such like.

'Suffer not thy mouth to cause thy flesh to sin; neither say thou before the angel that it was an error; wherefore should God be angry at thy voice and destroy the work of thine hands.' Ecclesiastes 5 s 6. It helps to remember that no matter how 'light' we were before incarnating on earth, due to our Free Will (see Chapter on God's Will and our Free Will) we can either gravitate towards the light or darkness. For example, if in a previous life we had been King Solomon, and before that Moses, it only takes one lifetime of unrepentant wickedness to blow the lot and end up back in the quagmire of the Lower Etheric.

THE PHYSICAL PLANE - is the most solid of all the dimensions and it is whilst on this plane that we experience the *illusion* of separation from our Spirit. However, we are very fortunate to have this chance to incarnate, since through the feeling of 'maybe this is all there is', our experiences feel very real, and because of this we have the maximum chance to shed much of our 'Karmic burden', enabling our 'Spirit' to develop and mature. Naturally, this is dependent on us learning from those experiences.

The Physical Plane is the only place in which every sort of Spirit - good, bad, Spiritually mature and immature can intermingle. Thus, we can communicate with, and influence or be influenced by a being from a different Ethereal Plane from ourselves. For example, Fully Ascended Beings from the Pure Spiritual Realm may 'risk all' and incarnate here to help in their love for God and His Creation -even the Son of God incarnated here. Also, our body gives tremendous protection to our Spirit, and consequently we have a wonderful chance to wake up and rise to the light if we so choose.

FOOTNOTE: There are 'mitigating circumstances' regarding our 'psyche' after our physical death, based wholly on the Laws of Karma, the principles of which are particularly discussed in the chapter on Suffering. For example, should a person be born or become mentally handicapped, then this will naturally give those people close to them some big Karmic challenges. This, combined with the fact they will have worked off a large amount of Karma themselves through such a life of suffering, will mean that they will reap the corresponding rewards at the end of their life. There is naturally a huge difference between a mental patient who is unaware of their condition, and somebody who becomes mentally ill from not facing up to their daily challenges and maybe turns to heavy drinking or drugs or anything so as to avoid looking at themselves. The latter type of mental illness is a result of emotions such as self-pity, neglect, rejection and so forth. These emotions combined result in the individual feeling that they are not able to take responsibility for their life. There are, of course, many degrees between a predominantly socially induced condition and a biological condition. Hence, only the Spirit of the individual in alignment with God's Will can know the true state of affairs - which is what matters. This concept is discussed throughout the book.

themselves whilst having an operation, or when people are very ill they may become confused, stating they sometimes find that they have two bodies, and if it's the Ethereal Body holding say a glass of water, the glass will fall onto the bed. As mentioned, the Ethereal Body becomes predominant in order to operate in the Ethereal Realm. Likewise, the physical body is predominant on earth, enabling the Spirit to operate in the Physical Realm.

The form of the Ethereal Body is determined by the Inner Density Law. The more 'earthly' we are after death, the more the Ethereal Body matches the physical body that was cast aside. Moreover, 'As a man thinketh in his heart, so is he.' Proverbs 23 vs 7. Thus, if we are 'young at heart', the Ethereal Body follows suit, no matter how old the person is when he/she dies. The lighter the Inner Density of the person after death, the more luminous the Ethereal Body will become, corresponding more and more to the shape, form and nature of the Spirit. It must be remembered that when I speak of Inner Density, I am speaking of the Inner Density of the Spirit, wrapped in its ethereal cloak.

THE PHYSICAL BODY: comprises the flesh and blood, which in 'biblical' terms is carnal. The brain, however, registers other aspects, such as thoughts and imagination, emotions, feelings and the five senses. It also has the ability to rationalise, deduce and analyse, which enables us to put into context our thought processes. Collectively all these components make up the Intellect. This enables us to interact with our environment. The Etheric has its own counterparts to these, which some may describe as psychic e.g. clairvoyants. These two bodies and all their functions are the Tools of the Spirit Self. Our Spirit speaks to us via our *'INTUITIVE PERCEPTION'*, that 'sings' to us from the heart and from there is registered by the brain. Also, our dreams can communicate messages from our Spirit (See Footnote).

Our Intuitive Perception is a very subtle force in the Karmic game. This helps to maintain the illusion of separation from who we really are, which makes our experiences seem all the more real (Karmic lessons are necessary so as to encourage our Spirit to grow, as mentioned). Our intuitive perception, being very subtle, means that it can be over in a split second. For example, when we meet someone for the first time, or see a friend who's hiding something, we may well get a quick 'impression'. More often than not we dismiss these initial thoughts, yet they sometimes prove to be correct at a later date. Likewise, when driving and approaching a blind bend, we may get a quick warning flash and slow down as a car coming the other way hurtles round on our side of the road. The most common one is if the telephone rings, we sometimes 'intuitively' know who it is.

The Spirit is one, whole, unified Self which animates the body, empowers the emotional and mental functions, and gives life to the 'Ego-Self'. The *EGO* is born at the same moment as the individual is born, and is made up of many, many 'selves':- There is a sad me, a happy me, an aggressive me, a stubborn me, a loving me, a vicious me and so on. In nature, 'ego' is our instinct of hunger, survival (fight or flight etc.) and procreation, whereby we live according to our needs. This is the True purpose of our ego. However, because of our over-developed Intellect in today's society (especially) this ego has become pampered, and most of us tend to indulge in excess beyond our natural needs, such as food (either too much - greed, or too little to keep fashionably thin - vanity), sex, and wanting what we cannot have. These combine to give us emotional extremes, such as anger, jealousy, envy, bitterness and feelings of depression.

Thus, the Ego-Self develops a false personality (persona) of its own if it dominates the Spirit, giving rise to the many base emotions. Our Ego-Self dies at physical death and our Spirit lives on - the degree of contamination corresponding to how we got on and all past experiences. Therefore, as the distorted Ego suffers, the Spirit matures. 'For he that soweth to his flesh shall of the flesh reap corruption; but he that soweth to the Spirit shall of the Spirit reap life everlasting.' Galatians 6 vs 8.

It is the Ego-Self when over dominant that grabs hold of Mammon. The ultimate fear of a pampered ego is death and pain. However, if our Spirit is in control, Mammon (all earthly goods of value - both material and monetary) can be used very effectively. Hence, we need to train our Ego-Self to 'listen' to our Spirit, since the Spirit is the origin of all impulses and the Ego-Self 'should' do exactly what it's told. Base emotions tell us that we have more soul searching to do and changes to make for our Spiritual Development. The correct balance between our Spirit and our Ego-Self is our objective. As in all things, this is down to each one of us individually.

If we just had a physical body and the pure Spirit Spark of God's Will (which is in all of us and tells us via our hearts and conscience when we're aligned or not - should we listen!), we would all gravitate straight to Heaven at Physical Death; i.e. the Saint would go to Heaven along with all the mass murderers and child molesters. This would of course make a mockery of all our suffering and Karmic lessons. Therefore, our Etheric Body makes sure we only gravitate to the level of corresponding Inner Density that gives our Spirit the 'correct' lessons for further development.

FOOTNOTE: DREAMS are a very good indicator of our 'Spiritual Progress'. Dreams contain messages, warnings and general information from our Spirit, and the less confused our dreams become, the more in alignment we tend to be with God's Will. This is a good reflection as to the state of our Intuitive Faculty which we may have been working on through meditation or sincere prayer. Sometimes we may get dreams of an identifiable situation, in which all the relevant people are clearly apparent. At other times, the message may come to us 'symbolically', not dissimilar to parables. In the case of the latter we have to work a little harder to decipher what the dream means for us, but it may reveal a deeper meaning and purpose. If our dreams are fear ridden, and contain nightmares - which may or may not recur, we are being told that there is something we need to look at in our lives and deal with.

AURAS - we all have round our bodies a protective energy field or Aura. This has been proven scientifically, although some psychics can see it without equipment. Auras are also 'reflective' of our inner state, and contain emanations of our physical, mental and emotional being. Their thickness, uniformity and colour give a good indication as to the state of the individual's health. For example, a lot of red in the aura denotes anger, and should our aura be thin in places or even have holes in it, then this is a reflection of a weakness, imbalance and/or illness.

TOOLS (PLUS 'GIFTS' AND 'SYSTEMS')

There are many thousands of 'Tools' used throughout the world, such as reading tea leaves, people's palms, crystal balls and so on. The definitions below refer to a few of the more common ones, of which I have some degree of personal experience.

Tools are exactly what the word suggests. For some people they are a means to an end in that they help us to understand more of the 'unseen'. This may then enable us to accept and come to terms with that which we can see around us and in our own lives. However, there are potential dangers (see Chapter on Tools later); a spade can be used effectively for digging the earth but, if we are careless, we may thump it down on our foot.

Also, the bigger the Tool, the more work we can get done, but the greater the potential danger to ourselves. For example, the difference in working with a handsaw and a chainsaw. With the proper training and gradual build up of solid foundations, skill and understanding a chainsaw can be used safely and effectively - provided we remain aware of its potential dangers and never get complacent and careless. Psychic tools and gifts work on exactly the same principles.

DIVINATION: To 'divine' is to find a solution or answer to any given matter/issue, through a particular process which often involves the use of certain tools or systems. Divination tools include Divining/Dowsing Rods, Tarot Cards, Runes, Crystal Balls and so on, and systems include such things as Numerology, Astrology or the Kabbalah/Tree of Life.

TAROT - a structured pack of cards used for Divinatory purposes (detailed in Chapter on Tools), whereby a general picture of past, present and future events can be built up, concerning such things as health, wealth, relationship ups and downs, beginnings and endings. Tarot cards can also reveal personal aspects to the seeker, such as their inner and outer state, motivation and desires, strengths and weaknesses, and Spiritual alignment.

The Tarot reader can use traditional spreads such as the Celtic Cross, or make up his own to give the desired information. However, I believe that the principal purpose of the Tarot is to reveal hidden Truths, preserved in pictorial forms which help us to gain a greater understanding of life and our part in Creation - both Physical and Spiritual. This concept is just touched on later, because a full picture would need a book of its own.

OUIJA BOARDS - consist of the letters of the alphabet arranged around a glass or object on a table. A group of people then attempt to get a Spirit to spell out a message. It is through this method that most of the horror stories we hear about occur, and it is this method which often (though not always), appeals to the younger generation who get a mischievous excitement out of dabbling with such things, and hence often attract the less agreeable 'Earthbound' Spirits. The problem with such devices as Ouija boards is not that they don't work, but that they sometimes do.

ASTROLOGY: This is a 'System' which can be used by Diviners, Astronomists and/or mathematical numerologists. Many books have been written on this subject but here I will give the briefest definition: When we are born, the star sign we take on, and the corresponding personality traits, is identified by which constellation of stars is directly behind the sun at the time of our birth. Each sign lasts approximately one month - the twelve signs of the Zodiac. The position of the moon at the *exact* time of birth, with whatever conglomerate of stars behind it (whether it be Cancer, Aries, Gemini etc.), determines the star sign we have 'in our Ascendancy', which exerts a degree of influence over us, but nothing like that of our 'sun' sign. This can be likened to a clock, where the twelve hour points mark the twelve signs of the Zodiac, so that where the hour hand points, this denotes our star sign (that is, in alignment with the earth and sun at birth), with the minute hand denoting our star sign in the Ascendancy (that is, in alignment with the earth and moon at birth).

REGRESSION - is when we are taken back to events that happened in the past, either in this life or past lives. This can be done either under hypnosis or in a state of semi-consciousness, similar to the state between sleeping and waking. The idea is to connect with an incident in the past which is still causing us deep emotional hurt and hence blocking our Spiritual progress in some way. Having 'connected' with the incident, whether it be abuse in childhood or being hanged in a past life, the person who is being regressed is encouraged to focus on the incident, allowing all the emotions to come to the surface expressing them in whatever way they wish. This can be very painful. They are then encouraged to forgive - themselves and others and *let go*.

If the exercise is completed successfully, the individual will feel considerably lighter and freer. However, it must be stressed that it doesn't matter if the individual feels they are letting go of an 'actual' past life experience, whether this is true or not.

The point is solely the clearing of deep emotional blockages which are present *now*.

As is the case in using any Tool or System, there are potential dangers. Hence, if there is the smallest doubt about the person who is regressing you and/or any fear at all, I believe that it is best not to do it.

If we are regressed in a semi-conscious state, we will have some measure of control. However, if fully hypnotised we will in some cases have no control over the proceedings. There are two main dangers of being hypnotised: Firstly, we don't necessarily know what is going to surface and if we're not in any control ourselves, the consequences could be damaging. Secondly, and more importantly, if we are in a hypnotised state, our Spirit is *bound*, and we have given up our Free Will not to God, but to the hypnotist. Should the hypnotist not fully bring us back into ourselves, even though he probably tries his best, our Spirit will still be partially bound and our Free Will will no longer be totally Free. In this case, the consequences to *both* parties, due to the laws of Karma, will not be too healthy, and may result in a marked slowing down of our Spiritual development as opposed to the desired speeding up.

There is, of course, no substitute for the daily lessons and tests 'life' presents to us. By boldly taking responsibility for ourselves and focusing inwardly during difficult times, we can bring our own blocks to the surface, then face up to and deal with them. This will no doubt involve a letting go of something or someone, and/or an aspect of our character which is not always easy. For example, if that means humbling ourselves before people or a person over whom we have always felt superior, or loving someone whom we've always hated, then this will necessitate a huge change in our character.

CLAIRVOYANCE/AUDIENCE/SENTIENCE and so on:-
These are the 'psychic' equivalents of our five senses. Some people are born clairvoyant, and they have to learn the right way of using such gifts in accordance with God's Will. This is because though they have been born with the gift, they have not necessarily been born with the discipline of their gift.

The psychic senses are the means by which messages are transmitted from the Spiritual, Ethereal and Physical environment to a medium. However, we are *all* of us mediums/ clair... something, in whatever form is most appropriate for us at the time. This is because we are all of us a Spirit in our own casings (as discussed earlier) and have an Intuitive Perception. Messages come to us in many forms, such as a 'very strong feeling' that we should do something - clairsentience, or visual pictures which reveal something to us when we're fully awake/ conscious or in dreams - clairvoyance. These pictures can either be realistic and depict the precise situation and people involved, or symbolic, in which case we need to interpret the symbolism ourselves.

GIFTS:- Everybody on Earth has a Gift, whether it be Spiritual, sport, a good joke teller, brilliant at sums, or just simply in our ability to give to others. However, it's up to us to find what the gift is and use it correctly. If the Spirit of God is omnipresent, does this not mean his energy is as much in a pack of cards as in a computer or church pew? *But it is always our* Personal Responsibility in everything we choose to do or use. The perfection of God's Will is that we only get exactly what we need for our Spiritual Growth, and hence there's no need to envy another who can see auras for example.

MEDIUMSHIP - 'Tuning in' to the Spirit of another who has 'passed over', in order to get a message which may help in some way. This 'other' may be a relative or friend. The medium can 'see' and/or 'hear' the one they are contacting because of the faculties of clairvoyance and clairaudience, for example, by 'seeing' the Ethereal body of the one contacted and 'hearing' what they have to say.

A sensible medium is firm and often 'bossy' with the Spirits who sometimes get over-excited at having made contact. However, the threat of 'cutting them off' soon brings them back into line to deliver the message - similar to ticking off a child. A poor medium, owing to their low level of Inner Density, will only be able to contact earth-orientated Spirits, which have all the corresponding potential dangers, as with *all the tools*. All such Spirits can really prove is the fact of life after death, and not much else, although some messages can be of benefit.

CHANNELLING - is when we calm ourselves into a meditative type state by shutting out all the normal clutter and banter which fills our minds, and allow the Spirit of another to speak *through* us. The idea being is we allow ourselves to be a channel, or 'tool' for a Spirit to communicate a message, over which we have little or no control. This is, of course, very similar to being a medium. The difference is that a medium speaks to, receives and interprets messages from the Spirit who is being contacted, whereas a channeller allows the Spirit to work through them, thereby allowing the enquirer to speak directly to the Spirit.

'Chanellers' have been referred to by many different names over the ages, such as 'Trance-mediums', and Prophets, although true Prophets didn't just contact any Spirit, but were

'Divinely Inspired' (see below). However, some mediums and channellers may flit between the two, so it is not always easy to tell the difference.

In certain cases a 'message' can be written. In these instances, the entity takes the body and guides the hand of the 'channeller', and in general, the handwriting, style and/or words used will correspond to the period in which the Spirit lived in their last incarnation. This is known as 'Automatic Writing'.

Some people refer to bringing in our 'Higher Selves' as channelling. Higher Selves means the Spirit Spark of pure Truth which abides in the heart of everyone of us. Once again, the aim is to empty our mind and body of emotions, personal feelings and desires, and focus on our perception of the Truth - pure and simple. The words 'Higher Self' imply that there is some part of us which enters from outside. However, I believe that the answers lie within and not without. Some feel our Higher Self enters (with the correct focus and concentration) through the top of our head or 'Crown', but to call this 'channelling' can be misleading, since channelling ourselves is not strictly channelling.

PROPHECY:- A 'True Prophet' is a 'channeller' of God, and according to the law of Inner Density, that means the only True Prophet to have lived was the Son of God - the one Being to have incarnated from God himself. Other Prophets or Servants of God's Will include Isaiah and John the Baptist, who were certainly Divinely inspired. They were often uneducated men who both foretold the coming of the Son of God and much else. It is through the prophets that God speaks to us with a voice and language we use everyday, whether it be of things happening in the past, present or future. A False Prophet is one who is the mouth piece of some being, Spirit or entity other than God, who is an impostor seeking self-gain and/or power.

AN OVERVIEW

When discussing subjects such as those contained in this book, it is important to realise that there are many different interpretations of how the human is composed, and even more on what happens to him afterwards. For example, some feel that the body is made up of the Physical Shell, which is also occupied by our Ethereal Body - our 'life force', or the living blueprint that shapes and activates our Physical Shell. In this case, our Astral Body is our instinctive/feeling Self - that which makes us like or dislike things/people, run away or fight and so on, and our Ego is our rational and moral Self, which through thought can make judgements and potentially rein us in when tempted. However, this is to be distinguished from the egotistical aspect of our 'lower' Ego - our selfish side - phew!

In this situation, it is felt that the Ethereal Body also 'shapes' the Physical. For example, if our 'life force' is retracted, gangrene can be the result, or if we are 'imbalanced', cancer may appear because the development and growth of cells is not controlled. Also, the Astral Body is the only medium which can transmit the experiences of the earth to the Ego/Spirit, such as feelings of love and beauty. At death, it is believed that the Physical and Ethereal bodies 'die' and the Astral and Ego live on, the Astral body gradually dying off over thirty odd years depending on the density of the individual. The length of astral death depends on how long it takes to work through the Karma of the previous life, actually 'experiencing again' the feelings of shame, guilt and so on, and come to terms with the lessons of that life. Naturally, there are many variations and differences of opinion on this theme - very oversimplified here!

As to the 'After Life', the word 'levels' can be misleading and fuel our egos if we're not careful, to make us feel that we're at a higher level than our neighbour. This is not humility (see later), and hence in reality it's more than likely the other way round! However, any such thinking is *not the point*, since we attract lessons/situations in this life appropriate for our Spiritual Growth, and likewise in the afterlife, we find ourselves in the appropriate surroundings giving us the appropriate lessons. I am a great believer in the concept of: 'As above so below', and: '*Thy will* be done on earth as it is in heaven'.

As mentioned, this book is based and drawn from my personal experiences. For example, when dealing with poltergeists a number of years ago, there was an overriding sense that they were trapped by a strong reluctance to *let go* of their own base emotions - mainly guilt. Hence, there was an air of prolonged sadness, combined with a certain childish mischievousness. In comparison, when doing mediumship work, the people coming through seemed to be very happy, and once they delivered their message couldn't get away quick enough back to where they'd just come from - unlike the 'denser' Spirits in the Lower Etheric who couldn't go anywhere.

It could possibly be more accurate to describe such levels in terms of different dimensions which can occupy the same space, perhaps unaware of the existence of one another, but distinguished by awareness and greater alignment with God. However, the 'principles' of the make up of the human being and the levels are more important than the exact details which I believe should be kept within sensible perspective. This is because the exploration of such details can overcomplicate, confuse and thereby distract us from living our *all important* physical lives, especially in the early stages of 'discovery', (it is easy to get over excited and 'blissy' when we begin to realise that there really is life after death). Hence, the 'levels' referred to in this book are simply a 'concept', no different to the Christian 'concept' of 'we rise up to heaven or we sink down into hell', and it's entirely down to us as to which way we gravitate.

I believe that the universe is very simple, and it is not hugely important whether we believe that we have two Ethereal bodies (a higher and a lower), an Astral body, two levels of Ego and a variety of specific Devils within us. As we acquire greater Knowledge of the underlying principles of the workings of the Universe, our Faith becomes stronger, and the more we feel God in our hearts and the more we desire and strive to be part of Him every moment of the day.

'As above so below', - the 'levels' referred to in this book can be likened to the Ocean and Sky, whereby the ocean bed is the Physical earth, the sea the Ethereal, and the blue sky above the Spiritual realm (the ultimate goal for all human Spirits). Space and Beyond in this analogy would be the realm of angelic beings, and way beyond them God, of whose 'perfection' we are none of us are worthy enough to begin to quantify:- 'And he said, Thou canst not see my face; for there shall no man see me, and live.' Exodus 33 vs 20.

To survive on the ocean bed we need to wear a heavy cloak, such as a divers bell. Likewise, whilst on earth, the densest plane of matter, we need to wear a dense physical cloak for our Spirit to survive in and work. The higher we rise towards the surface of the Ocean, the lighter our wet suit needs to be and the less baggage we need to carry in the form of oxygen cylinders. This is because the pressure/density decreases as we near the surface. We can also see and feel the light and warmth when near the surface as compared to being in pitch darkness at the lower levels. However, to rise out of the Ocean into the sky, we need to have shed our cloaks and let go of all

48

our baggage.

Another analogy is fish. Certain mammals and crustaceans live and move between very specific levels of depth suited to their particular nature and density. Some crustaceans and shell fish live on the ocean bed, where they survive due to their very thick shells, which allows them to take the pressure. Above this there are fish whose bodies are again designed to take the pressure; also because it's pitch dark at such depths, they don't have eyes, or their eyes are very underdeveloped, since they're not used!

Nearer to the surface, there are whales which can only swim down to a certain depth, and need to come to the surface for air. Similar to dolphins, they can leap out of the water, but gravity and their 'casing' ensure that they return quickly to their correct/suitable surroundings. Smaller fish, such as Cod and Mackerel, survive in bands just below the surface. There are, of course, many thousands of species all surviving at different depths.

'As above so below', - the depth to which a fish and its counterparts can survive and the proximity from the surface to which it can rise (with some even reaching the surface), is determined by the species - like attracts like, similarity of body denseness and hence equilibrium/type of species. As mentioned they oscillate up and down but only within very specific boundaries. Otherwise the individual would perish if it went into waters which were too deep or too shallow for it to handle naturally. For example, should a Mullet or Jelly Fish be washed up on the beach it will die, having become exposed to a completely different environment. The sky above the ocean comprises the air and light of pure untainted Spirit in this analogy, and all living creatures need a certain amount of this in order to survive. Therefore, the bodies of all living things in the Ethereal and on the Physical are adapted to breathe 'air' through the Ethereal/Physical medium that is right for it. As is the case with 'pressure', should the fish find itself in an environment of too little air or too much air it will not survive. Likewise, should we try to take in too much 'light' (or overdo the 'darkness') for our bodies, Physical and Ethereal, i.e. try to hurry and over-accelerate our natural progress, we will frazzle.

Spiritual Development is like climbing a ladder, in that we can only progress from the first rung to the second when we can stand solidly on the first rung in all conditions. A seedling raised in a greenhouse can be planted outside when weather conditions are right, and it will thrive. If it has been allowed to develop too far in artificial conditions before being planted out, it will be much more likely to perish. This is because it will have been 'accelerated' to expecting Summer conditions, so that the lower temperatures, sudden changes of weather conditions, gales and driving rain that occur in Spring would prove fatal. Likewise, a plant growing in dark surroundings, exposed to only a small shaft of light, will rapidly grow towards the source of that light, but the stem will be weak and the roots will be shallow, so it will eventually fall.

Therefore, progression must be natural. For example, if an individual decides to do Mediumship work using artificial aids such as hypnotism to hasten their progress on to another rung, all sorts of problems may arise. This is because we may not have the necessary grounding, stability, experiences and natural protection against potential adversaries (such as Lower Etheric undesirables). Likewise, with Tarot, looking for answers and understanding by endlessly flipping out the cards, will cause more confusion and possible harm if we've tried to skip a rung or two.

The above type situations can be likened to building up artificial muscle by intensively pumping iron. When we slow down or stop, such muscle rapidly turns to flab. There is a distinct difference between this, and a labourer who works long hours in any conditions over a number of years, and who becomes physically strong and remains so come what may. Hence, our Spiritual Development/Progress can be likened to Snakes and Ladders, whereby as we progress up the rungs, there will always be snakes at every stage which try to tempt us, expose and exploit our weak spots, so we slide back to the rung below, or sometimes back to the ground with a hefty thud!

2.GOD'S WILL AND OUR FREE WILL

It might appear that if God is 'All present, powerful and knowing', it is His Will that the world is a place of suffering. How frequently do we interpret the adage, 'nothing moves without Divine Intent', as God himself directly giving us suffering. In this state we find ourselves asking questions such as, 'How can this be God's love?' And, no doubt we tell God what we think of him! It is easy to blame another if we feel that we have been treated wrongly by forces outside our control. The clue is that God in His Love gave man *free will* to live and work in accordance with 'His Will' or not. The 'problem' is that most of us are afraid to seriously look into and know God's Will, in case it doesn't tie in with our own desires.

Free Will means that we can either do harm or good, go wrong or right - our choice. Hence, Free Will has made evil possible. So why did God give man Free Will, and the opportunity to create all the suffering, wars and tragedy that is common place now, and throughout History, when he could have created us as simple beings of love - truly in his own likeness? To start with a world of beings that worked like robots or machines would hardly be worth creating. Hence, God has created the perfect system giving all of us the opportunities to prove ourselves to Him by voluntarily giving up our self to live according to His Will (discussed later in chapter). Having experienced the lows we will fully appreciate the ecstasy of love and joy once we submit ourselves to Him with all our being. This is Freedom. We get many a taste of this in our daily lives as we overcome challenges and gradually let go of our earthly attachments and desires.

God knew what would happen if man used his Free Will the wrong way (discussed later in this chapter - section on 'Destiny'), yet still it seems decided it was worth the risk. On looking around at the harm and hurt people inflict upon their neighbour, we many of us may disagree with God and even get angry with him for creating such a system. Such thinking could prove a major stumbling block for us. This is because God is the source of all our energy, understanding and reasoning. Not only is it impossible for Him to be wrong and us right in even the minutest way, but disagreeing with Him will simply stall our Spiritual progress by blocking out His love and the answers from entering us. It is the same as cutting off the branch we're sitting on.

No matter what happens to us, our family, friends and countrymen, we can choose to remain in a state of love, humility, and forgiveness, or allow our base emotions to dictate our thoughts and actions. This book is intended to give some practical examples to help in maintaining the former state in our daily situations. Likewise, should this book, or any other, hit a nerve and throw up a base emotion, then this is simply showing us an area within ourselves on which we can work if we want to - in the same way people and situations induce such emotions.

When we take a step and make any decision, this will result in Karma, either good or bad. If the returning Karma is good, having tackled our challenge in accordance with God's Will, we will have worked off some of our 'Karmic baggage'. This will result in a lightening of our inner density by 'reaping what we've sown' from our 'good' deeds. Both are Karmically related, and an example of this is given in the final Chapter, in the section on Molestation, Violation and Abuse. Conversely, if we deal with the situation 'incorrectly', by succumbing to the temptations to satisfy our own desires, this will result in a further build up of our Karmic load. Therefore, before making a decision it will certainly help to ask 'what would God want me to do', and offset that against our personal desires (examples of the difference are given throughout this book).

'No blade of grass is blown without Divine intention.' The Laws of Attraction and Return means that whatever is happening in our lives and wherever we are is no coincidence. Our Spirit, through the filter of our personality 'attracts' every situation to help us shed our Karmic load and lighten our inner density. Our Free Will only applies to how we ourselves deal with the situation, but the Karma we receive, good or bad, will affect the next set of lessons we attract. Most of our daily 'coincidences' involve the gathering of information to help us deal with something or somebody (Karmically related), with us somehow reciprocating the favour at the same time.

Life is therefore a game of give and take. Should we make a decision which takes us off our path and on to a Spiritual tangent, we will attract situations to get us back on track in order to move up to the next rung of the Spiritual ladder. This will take as long or short a time as we allow, due to our Free Will. As we mature and become more aware in every moment of our day, we will see this process at work in our lives.

'Living' as fully as possible in every second of our lives doesn't mean we should totally 'bliss out' and not make any plans for the future. Whatever job or work we are doing, it is vital that we work as hard and with as much enthusiasm and effort as possible or we will not learn the lessons that we are there to learn. This principle is discussed fully in the Chapter on Work, but the concept of the 'more you put into it the more you get out of it', is equally applicable to our Spiritual Growth, particularly since our Spiritual progress is one hundred per cent related to how we live our daily lives.

However, nowadays, possibly more than ever, it is vital to remain flexible and be accepting, prepared for and alive to change, because our Spirit in alignment with God's Will may demand that we go on a different path to the one we'd planned. Should we be in a job where we have had all the 'experiences' we came to learn and/or given all that we came to give for the benefit, in whatever form, of others and the company, our Spirit will then demand a change. This is because stagnation is Spiritually painful. If we shut our ears to these demands due to our insecurities and fear of change, our Spirit will attract all sorts of situations to encourage us to let go. For example, it may be that no matter how hard we try we won't achieve anything and will end up feeling like we're banging our heads against a brick wall.

Conversely, when on the right track and doing what we 'should be doing' i.e. of maximum benefit for others, our surroundings and our own Spiritual growth, then everything slots into place. In other words, we do get genuine help from the Universe - via the Four Laws. For example, should we suddenly need to talk to a specific person then they will 'miraculously' appear or ring up, or if we need some money badly, then just the right amount will 'appear', often from an unexpected source. Also, our day will be packed full of wonderful little coincidences which help us get the maximum done. By looking out for such things in our daily lives we will: (a) get an accurate indication as to whether we're doing what is best for our Spiritual growth or if we're fighting against something we know we should be doing, and (b) begin to get a clearer picture of the Laws of the Universe in operation. It is possible to visualise these laws as some huge, perfect, eternal computer in complete control, creating the ideal situations, meetings, confrontations, suffering and so on, in which every one of us has our own ideal opportunities to develop Spiritually, if we choose to!

Therefore, there is no such thing as events occurring outside of Karmic Law, because as mentioned, when we get side-tracked, we still get the ideal help for our Spirit via challenges and suffering which help us to 'grow'. We reap what we sow in every moment of our lives.

Because all our experiences are interconnected, when one of us goes down a 'tangent' - owing to Free Will, this will affect the lessons and experiences of others who come into contact with us. If the experiences others receive from us are ideal for their Spiritual Growth (in the same way as the experiences we gain from them are ideal for ours), this will necessitate a reorganisation in the giant 'computer' of God's Will. This could even have global repercussions if we think of all the people they then come into contact with and so on, which is the meaning behind the Eastern philosophy of 'when a butterfly moves its wings in one part of the globe, a hurricane can be the result on the other side.'

It must be remembered that God's Universal Laws are incomparably more intelligent than anything, computer or otherwise, that could be designed by man. God's Laws are perfect, work automatically and can never make a mistake. Therefore, the importance of sowing seeds of love instead of those of hatred, because of the potentially far reaching knock-on effects, takes on a whole new meaning.

When *God's Will* is referred to in the text, I am referring simply to the above Four Laws, which can be likened to the *rays* of the sun but *not* the sun itself - which in this context is likened to God - whereby despite His involvement in what goes on below, He Himself is *untainted* and remains *pure* and *perfect*.

This principle is suggested in the Parable of the Vineyard, Matthew 21 vs 33 - 42:- 'There was a certain householder (God) which planted a vineyard, and hedged it round about, and dug a wine press in it, and built a tower (his creation), and let it out to husbandmen (God made man), and *went into a far country*: (God having created the beautiful perfect universe takes an overview leaving simply His Will imprinted upon everything).' However, man due to his Free Will, opts in an overall sense for the base temptations, and kills the servants (prophets) who are sent and even kills the 'Son of the Householder', until the householder steps in again on the Day of Judgement (See Footnote) destroying the wicked and saving the good 'which shall render him the fruits in their seasons' (align with God's Will). The point being:- 'The stone which the builder rejected, the same is become the head of the corner.' Matthew 21 vs 42.

An example of universal help is Peter's deliverance from prison in Acts 12, in that had Peter remained in prison, he would no doubt have been put to death. The angel coming down from Heaven, freeing his chains and opening the gates whilst putting all the guards to sleep is a miracle; a little more obvious than the miracles that occur in our daily lives, but no different in principle.

Peter *voluntarily* surrendered his whole *self* to God and aligned his Free Will to *choose* to do that of God's and not his own. This is the objective/goal of every human Spirit on earth and is called *faith*. Having placed himself totally in God's hands to do God's work, he reaped what he had sown via the Law of Attraction, because when he was in jail he had the requisite 'lightness' for help to come to him in the form of an angel. He was also at a stage of Spiritual maturity that he could recognise that it as an angel. This, of course, is an example of good Karma, but Peter had worked very, very hard throughout his life to get to such a stage of God centredness/purity.

'He that findeth his life shall lose it: and he that loseth his life for my sake shall find it;' Matthew 10 vs 39. Peter 'chose' to do God's Will when he left his family to follow Christ. However, he did not submit himself entirely to God's Will until he had denied Christ three times. From thereon he was prepared to die for God and his salvation was complete. Once Peter had demonstrated his absolute Faith in God, the chains that bound him to any earthly desires and needs which could prevent God from entering his heart, fell away. This same principle applies to *all* aspects of our daily lives, but due to the Laws of Attraction and Return, the stronger our Faith (discussed in Chapter on Faith), the bigger the miracles in our lives.

To submit our whole self to God, like Peter did eventually, is the hardest thing we any of us can achieve whilst on earth. This is our sole means to salvation/heaven, and every test we get in our daily lives - good or apparently bad are there to help us move towards this state. The vast majority of us are like Ananias and his wife Sapphira in Acts 5. They sold a possession and 'kept back a part of the price, and brought a certain part and laid it at the apostles' feet'. They both then in turn implied that they had given the full value of their possession. However, Peter, in the same way as God, saw straight through their lie pointing out that 'thou hast not lied unto men, but unto God'. They then both respectively had a heart attack and died.

The point of being True to God in the submission of Self naturally hit home hard to those who witnessed this event. As mentioned, our base emotions, expectations, pride and ego resulting from our carnal and materialistic earthly attachments and desires show us, and God, the extent we're not aligned to the Light.

There is a perennial combat between light and darkness, between the flesh and the Spirit. Human nature stained by actual sin on the one hand, and Grace urging us ever upwards on the other, cannot be friendly companions along the way. One of the two must disappear.

An individual who craves worldly honours and pleasures freely offered on all sides, whose longings and volitions gravitate towards the earthly, who dissipates himself in every fashion, seeking to gratify his sensual, worldly leanings, will never succeed in acquiring a taste for God's light and love. A state of Grace will always allude us when our focus is like this, and we will remain a slave of external things with a base, materialistic outlook.

Somebody who strives for Grace will utilise with resolute determination and dexterity the weapons that alone can safeguard a life of God-centredness against our most insidious foes - that of temptations and lukewarmness. 'And if thy hand (foot and/or eye) offend thee, cut it off: it is better for thee to enter into life maimed, than having two hands to go into hell, into the fire that never shall be quenched.' Mark 9 vs 43. For example, hair these days does seem to be a vanity thing for most of us. Beautiful models do tend to have beautiful hair and are therefore judged favourably as a result. Should we become reliant on our hair as an important part of our outward appearance to gain approval at work, socially and with the opposite sex - in other words to assist in our attainment of purely earthly goals at the expense of Spiritual goals, Christ is encouraging us to cut if all off. The more we become 'naked' before our fellow man the more naked we become before God, which allows Him further access into our hearts.

In the light of the above we may ask how our 'Free Will' and 'Freedom' are affected? Free Will, as mentioned, means we always have the choice of doing good or evil regarding everything in our lives. However, if we interpret Freedom as being able to say, do and think whatever we want and our volition is for our Spiritual Growth, then there are very tight boundaries within this framework. This is because to embrace God in our hearts means we must sacrifice everything - all earthly desires and attachments, to Him:- 'Straight is the gate, and narrow is the way, which leadeth unto life, and few there be that find it.' Matthew 7 vs 14. To be 'Free' our hearts need to be fully open. The *only* way we can open our heart is to open it to God. This means we need to make ourselves a slave to God, willingly embracing and embodying all the 'limitations' discussed in this book. This will give us our maximum opportunity for 'Freedom' whilst on earth. Therefore, taking the popular interpretation, there is no such thing as Freedom.

God is love. It is possible for us to overcome all obstacles for the love of God and to keep our heart free enough for the genuine love of God to dwell within us. It is feasible only at the cost of sacrifice, as mentioned. This will mean a constant, active, daily battle against not only our obvious faults and tendencies, but also the disordered attachments lurking in the background, clinging to the tendrils of the unwary heart. It is relatively easy to see the big problems within ourselves and our lives, and have a fair idea of how we should deal with them and understand that there is a need to do so. However, our passing daily thoughts - whether they be carnal, aggressive, envious and so on, are far harder to pin down and tackle. How often do we casually just let them continually come and go treating them as though 'they don't really matter or count'. If we resolutely try to conquer these attachments we will grow in strength. Cultivating the love of God in our hearts in this way may seem laborious, but it will have to be done sometime. Self-love with its cravings for comfort and sensual gratification, for praise and respect, clinging to others and hoping for everything from them, relaxes its hold reluctantly and only after stout resistance.

'Love suffereth long, and is kind; love envieth not; love vaunteth not itself, is not puffed up, Doth not behave itself unseemly, seeketh not her own, is not easily provoked, thinketh no evil; Rejoiceth not in iniquity, but rejoiceth in the truth; Beareth all things, believeth all things, hopeth all things, endureth all things.' 1 Corinthians 13 vs 4 - 7. When we have truly given our heart to God, nothing from tribulation or distress, famine or nakedness, danger, persecution or the sword can separate us from Him. This is what is meant by the 'Denial of Self', and is the 'Freedom' Peter achieved by the end of his life.

Since our Karma shapes every situation in our lives to give us the tests we need, what of *destiny*? 'To everything there is a season, and a time to every purpose under the heaven: A time to be born, and a time to die.' Ecclesiates 3 vs 1, 2. If we take this verse literally, it could be argued that every test we meet in our lives is a 'Destiny' point. This would imply that all our challenges are written in the Heavens and ingrained into our very beings before we are born. As a result, the importance of our Free Will would dramatically reduce, because if we were 'choosing' to align rapidly with God's Will and we encountered a preset series of Karmic lessons, our tests of Destiny wouldn't prove any real challenge and thereby not help us to move forward Spiritually. Likewise, should an A Level student have to revise for and sit an Eleven Plus exam it would be utterly pointless. The same principle, in reverse, applies should our progress be very slow.

Not only would such a state of affairs make a mockery of the point of our Free Will, but we'd all either be frustrated or totally overpowered. However, if we open our eyes, we will see that this is not the case, because we will realise that the challenges we receive do not push us beyond the limit with which we can cope, if sometimes only just, to help us to 'grow'. This is provided we deal with our test 'correctly' (discussed in Chapter on Fear).

We therefore need to be very careful when saying that something is Destiny. Should we meet somebody or find ourselves in a situation and a huge coincidence happens, we may feel that this is part of our Destiny. However, should we wish to interpret this as Destiny, it should be 'destiny' with a small 'd', because it is the same as our Spirit attracting the ideal circumstances for our Karmic lessons and the Karma of others, and it is governed by how we have coped with our experiences up until then.

Destiny (big D) means that something happens which comes directly from God and is implemented by Him to maintain His overall 'Divine Plan'/Destiny for mankind and the world as a whole. This is what is meant by .... 'a time to every purpose *under the heaven*', on a global scale. For example, in the Parable of the Vineyard it is written:- 'And when the time of the fruit drew near, he sent his servants to the husbandmen, that they might receive the fruits of it.' Matthew 21 vs 34. These servants/prophets were duly 'beaten, killed and stoned'. Hence, to maintain His Divine plan it was necessary for God to send his Son to earth and 'die' for the sake of mankind. This was a 'Destiny' point for mankind, because the message of Christ is still very much alive today (albeit not always in the way he meant it!).

It had become clear to God many years prior to Christ's arrival that it would be necessary to send him because man had so blatantly abused his Free Will and succumbed to all the temptations of the earth. Hence, 'For His love for mankind, God gave his only begotten Son.' The Prophets, such as David and Isaiah, communicated this message from God of the coming of the Messiah. However, if man had been aligning with God's Will, God would not have sent his Son to earth, because it wouldn't have been necessary.

'Logically' it is easy to see why it was necessary for Christ to be put to Death by man. This was in order to emphasise irrevocably the full impact of the human race's overall rejection of God's Truth, in favour of carnal lust, materialistic objectives and desires over and above a Spiritual focus, plus the need to be admired, adored, looked up to by others and so forth. The fact that the prophets were 'given' the details concerning Christ many years in advance, with Christ duly fulfilling these scriptures, gives further impact to this sad reflection on the state of mankind. Such shocking revelations should be enough to wake us up, but whatever, the simple 'way' of Truth is now quite clearly marked and is there for all of us to see - if we want to.

Destiny therefore only comes into play at God's discretion, whereby he uses somebody as a 'tool' to help the masses and keep the Destiny of the world on course. Because of this not even the angels know His complete plan. For example, we most of us know that the Day of Judgement (see Footnote) is on its way, however:- 'But of that day and that hour knoweth no man, no, not the angels which are in heaven, neither the Son, but the Father.' Mark 13 vs 32.

We might well argue that if God influences the overall Destiny of mankind and He is a God of love, it is His fault all the suffering and wars happen! However, as mentioned, God in His love for us gave us Free Will from the very beginning. For Adam and Eve the rules were very simple and made totally clear to them, whereby they could do whatever they liked, provided they didn't eat of one particular tree:- 'But of the tree of knowledge of good and evil, thou shalt not eat of it: for in the day that thou eatest thereof thou shalt *surely die.*' Genesis 2 vs 17.

In the beginning, there was almost certainly two possible courses for 'mankind'; *Path A* bound by the Law of Love, and *Path B* bound by the Law of Karma. The ideal option would have been to embrace God's Laws of humility, unconditional love, love thy neighbour as thyself and so on. However, the tune was quickly set when the serpent talked Eve and through Eve, Adam, into eating the 'Forbidden Fruit'; '… ye shall be as gods, knowing good and evil.' Genesis 3 vs 5.

It became clear to God even from this early stage that earthly desires were going to dominate man's thinking. Hence, there was just one path open for mankind, whereby only out of suffering would he 'listen' and gain wisdom and understanding and thereby grow 'Spiritually'. Goodness knows how many of us are old souls and have incarnations going back to the early part of history and are thus directly responsible for mankind being in its current predicament. That's some 'Karma' to work off !

God could not contain His initial frustration, fury and sadness (Genesis 3 vs 14 - 24) when He saw that man was going to opt for Path B instead of Path A - knowing all the suffering that was to come as a result. If man had chosen Path A, then the ten commandments given to Moses would not have been necessary, (similar to the 'necessity' of Christ coming to earth), because if we had been the embodiment of love; then lust, possession, murder, theft, selfishness and so on wouldn't have even entered our heads.

Hence, when WE created this path, God could see clearly the large global events playing themselves out - in other words, as far as God is concerned, the Global Wheel of Destiny has already happened. This is not that hard to comprehend once we start to realise how many trillion times more wise God is than any of us - being Omnipresent, Omnipotent and Omniscient. As mentioned, in His love for us, He 'went into a far country', leaving His Universal Laws in place and has allowed us to keep our Free Will, whereby through the tragedies and wars we have caused and are causing, we are directly shown where we are going wrong and how we should change the way we live our lives. This is discussed in detail in the chapter on Suffering.

He has given us further help via His prophets and His son, so as to keep the Global Wheel turning. The combination of the Prophets 'being given' information about important Global events, sometimes thousands of years into the future; the giving of His Son who provided us with the details of God's love - Path A; and the Karmic lessons from the suffering and sleaze all around us, should be enough proof for us to seek to radically change our lifestyles. He can't give us anymore without undermining the whole fabric of this current Karmic cycle based on our Free Will.

So what of D/destiny in terms of our place, race and date of birth and time and cause of death? As mentioned, the family and culture into which we are born is ideal for our Spiritual lessons and we for the lessons of others. This means that the body we take in whatever circumstances is correct for our individual Karmic needs, related to what we've done in our past - destiny little 'd'. Likewise, the time and cause of our physical death is determined by our Free Will exerted when dealing with the various challenges and situations in our lives. The benefits to our Spirit of suffering and even dying as a result of illness is discussed in the Chapter on Suffering.

Our Spirit attracts what it needs for its growth, which is determined by how we're progressing Spiritually or not during our lives - our individual Free Choice. Therefore, our time and cause of death, whether it be a sudden accident, heart attack, prolonged illness or simply 'old age', is Karmically related to the seeds we've sown throughout our lives. Hence, our Death is destiny little 'd', but is in accordance with God's Will (Karma) ... 'a time to every purpose *under the heaven*: A time to be born, and a time to die.' In this context, death only refers to the death of our body.

The world as it is now is a result of our whole history up to and including the present. If we point an accusing finger at anyone including God, then we haven't begun to fathom the *extent of our personal responsibility to ourselves, other people and creation.* To take responsibility means we need to be aware of our every thought, word and action, and acknowledge to ourselves and God when we make a mistake. By acknowledging in humble repentance the consequences of our mistakes we grow in knowledge, understanding and wisdom, and when we reap the benefits and blessings from sowing seeds of love and truth, these moments become our next step up towards paradise. Hence, Free Will is truly a precious gift from God, and is our means of Spiritual Ascension. 'Likewise joy shall be in heaven over one sinner that repenteth, more than over ninety nine just persons which need no repentance.' Luke 15 vs 7, re. The Prodigal Son.

Man has fundamentally abused his 'Free Will' over the ages as mentioned, and consequently it is *not God* who has created this sordid sleaze, suffering and wars - *we have*. God is love, and his creation is meant to be a place of love, giving and happiness; but love also means *justice*, in that His faultless Will is upheld at all times in irrevocable fairness. Hence, God has made the perfect system which works in such a way that we actually punish or reward ourselves. Through the interaction of our Free Will with God's Laws, we make our own happiness or misery.

'You can run but you can't hide.' Due to the omnipresence of God's Laws, every experience of our lives is ingrained upon our souls and played back to us at Physical Death at which time *we judge ourselves* by what we have done or not done, in accordance with God's Will - the Four Laws. This is a time, as discussed in the section on the Lower Etheric, when we cannot hide because every aspect of ourselves is exposed as clear as crystal in the light of God. If the shame or guilt or bitterness are so appalling to us, and we lack the courage to face up to ourselves, it is understandable why some of us choose to plunge into the darkness of the Lower Etheric, where we think we 'can't be seen'.

This ties in with many cases of so called 'near death experiences', when a collection of images of a person's life flashes by at great speed and they are sometimes given the *choice* of going down the 'Tunnel of light' or the murkier tunnel back to Earth. Some people are told that they must return due to the importance of the Karmic experience for them and those close to them. Either way, if a person returns to earth, it means that they still have more work they can do: For example, it may be to help their close friends and relatives, who would have completely gone to pieces had they passed on originally, to come to some sort of understanding and acceptance of themselves, thereby helping them to find the strength to keep going. Such unconditional giving receives the corresponding Reciprocal Action and lightening of Inner Density.

Free Will is exactly what it says, and because of this no matter how pure we may think we are, we are always vulnerable to temptation. For example, Jesus in the Garden of Gethsemane hinted at his 'Free Will':- 'If it be possible, let this cup pass from me,' Matthew 26 vs 39, hoping and willing that he might not have to go through the pain of his crucifixion. However, his next words were: 'nevertheless not as I will, but as thou wilt,' and reaffirmed moments later with conviction:- 'If this cup may not pass away from me, except I drink it, *thy will be done*.' Verse 42.

The warning and test for any Christian/good person who understands this is:- 'Watch and pray, that ye enter not into temptation: the Spirit indeed is willing, but the flesh is weak.' Matthew 26 vs 41. Whilst incarnate in our physical body, we and our Free Will will be tested until the very end - even Christ was no exception:- 'My God, my God, why hast thou forsaken me?' Mark 15 vs 34.

FOOTNOTE: THE DAY OF JUDGEMENT. Many Cultural, Religious and Spiritual groups believe that we're nearly at the end of this current Karmic cycle, because the prophets' and Christ's warning signs leading up to the 'Day of Judgement' are currently being fulfilled, with 'nation rising against nation, plagues, earthquakes, hurricanes, and floods' now commonplace throughout the world. Whether Judgement Day occurs in our current lifetime or afterwards none of us know, 'But of that day and that hour knoweth no man, no, not the angels which are in heaven, neither the Son, but the Father.' Mark 13 vs 32. There have been many people in recent years who have felt they've received a message that the 'end of the world is nigh' on such and such a day at a certain time and gathered groups of people to mountain tops in a blaze of publicity, only to sheepishly climb back down and return to their homes when nothing happens!

However, there is a sense of urgency to align with God's Will (even if Judgement Day doesn't happen in our lifetimes for all the other obvious reasons discussed in this book), because Judgement Day will come when we least expect it. 'For as in the days that were before the flood they were eating and drinking, marrying and giving in marriage, until the day that Noah entered into the ark. And knew not until the flood came, and took them all away; so shall also the coming of the Son of Man be.' Matthew 24 vs 38, 39. (The Son of Man coming to earth will occur on the Day of Judgement).

Until that time we will all keep flitting between physical incarnations and the Ethereal Realm. The bodies we take, in whatever circumstances, and the level in the Ethereal Realm to which we gravitate in between times, being dictated by the 'fruits we sow' governed by the Four Laws, as discussed. This is provided, of course, we don't manage to attain the state of purity necessary for us to enter into heaven and thereby free ourselves from this Karmic cycle once and for all. '*Let both* (the tares and the wheat) grow together until the harvest: and in the time of harvest I will say to the reapers, Gather ye together first the tares and bind them in bundles to burn them: but gather the wheat into my barn.' Matthew 13 vs 30. 'As therefore the tares are gathered and burned in the fire; so shall it be in the end of this world. The Son of Man shall send forth his angels, and they shall gather out of his Kingdom all things that offend, and them which do iniquity; And shall cast them into a furnace of fire: there shall be wailing and gnashing of teeth. Then shall the righteous shine forth as the Sun in the Kingdom of their Fathers. Who hath ears to hear, let him hear.' Matthew 13 vs 40 - 43.

The Day of Judgement is *serious*. It marks the end of this Karmic cycle of Free Will. Should we be one of the 'tares' we will meet with *death*, whereby we will be stripped of all our experiences in our current life, past lives and the ethereal world, as symbolised by the repeated referrals to 'fire and brimstone'. Our Spirit spark will then return to square one, having been stripped of all aspects of its personality and experiences, and have to start the whole Karmic cycle again as a totally new individual. This is the time and meaning of 'Spiritual Death' and it will be a very painful process, 'And in those days shall men seek death, and shall not find it; and shall desire to die, and death shall flee from them.' Revelations 9 vs 6.

As to the exact timing of Judgement Day, it could be argued that if this 'Day' was written by God 'in the beginning', then where is His love when we and all our Karmic experiences are annihilated - this particularly if mankind had been some way to aligning with His Will? If the world had chosen to align with God's Will, then Judgement Day would be a time of joy, celebration and happiness. Even though we may lose our current physical bodies, and we are all 'grains of wheat', we would fully understand that our all important Spirits are eternal. The 'joy' would result from the knowledge that we would never again have to live in a world where needless suffering exists. Sadly this is not the case and even if Judgement Day is fixed, we will all have had plenty of lifetimes and opportunities to welcome God's light, love and Truth over and above all our earthly desires. Therefore, God is still very much performing an act of love even if we are one of the tares - what is the point of going on indefinitely when we refuse to wake up no matter what opportunities are given to us?

When 'The Day' comes, if we have not sincerely and humbly repented, it will be too late. However, up to and including the eleventh hour we all of us still have a chance of attaining Salvation. For example, one of the thieves crucified with Christ, having rebuked the other thief for asking Christ to, 'save thyself and us', asked Jesus, 'Lord, remember me when thou comest into thy kingdom. And Jesus said unto him, Verily I say unto thee, Today shalt thou be with me in paradise.' Luke 23 vs 42,43.

If we take the attitude of, 'in that case I'll carry on indulging myself in earthly pleasures until such time as I see the Son of Man coming down, when I'll sincerely repent and humble myself before God', we automatically condemn ourselves to being one of the tares. '...But and if that evil servant shall say in his heart, My lord delayeth his coming: And should begin to smite his fellow servants, and to eat and drink with the drunken; The Lord of that servant shall come in a day when he looketh not for him, and in an hour that he is not aware of, And shall cut him asunder, and appoint him his portion with the hypocrites: there shall be weeping and gnashing of teeth.' Matthew 24 vs 42-51.

God sees our hearts, and when the thief crucified with Christ humbly gave his whole self and being to Christ, he was immediately welcomed with open arms. This is an example of God's forgiveness and love for mankind, because even dictators, war-mongers and mass murderers have a chance up until the last minute. Spiritual Death therefore only occurs on

Judgement Day, but the more we are entrenched in the 'things of the earth' at this time or in the dense, darker realms of the Lower Etheric, the less chance we will have of survival.

Therefore, unless our Spirit is pure enough to rise out of the Physical and Ethereal planes during this Karmic cycle, its objective is to be 'mature' enough by the time Judgement Day arrives so that we are one of the grains of wheat as opposed to one of the tares. God draws the line, so it is impossible for any man to begin to quantify what that will be. 'I am Alpha and Omega, the beginning and the ending, saith the Lord, which is, which was and which is to come, the Almighty.' Revelations 1 vs 8.

TWO EXAMPLES OF GOD'S WILL

THE TEN COMMANDMENTS: The Four Laws are the same as the ten commandments but hopefully will help to clarify the consequences when those commandments are abused. For example, 'Thou shalt not steal' - if we do steal, we reap the Reciprocal Action and our Inner Density becomes more contaminated; like attracts like - we naturally attract and mix with those of like minds; and, the law of equilibrium - we are responsible for an increase in the darkness around us, 'fuelling' the denser forces of a like nature in the Lower Etheric. It is important to realise that the ten commandments relate to all elements of our lives. 'Thou shalt not steal', refers not just to the theft of physical things, but also to psychological things and so on.

One of Jesus' commands was to 'Love thy neighbour as thyself'. We are here to learn, and it is through the increase of knowledge and understanding of the 'Word of God' in our hearts that makes us bow down irresistibly to the perfection of God's creation. In so doing, we will recognise all humans as part of a uniform oneness, and as a result will not feel anything but love and compassion for our fellow man. Such love in our heart lightens the density within us with positive Reciprocal Action - and vice versa!

GOSSIPING: Here is an example of how the laws work in day to day life: Gossiping, i.e. any undermining idle 'chat', malicious or otherwise, is something of which the world is full and which we have all been guilty of doing. A person gossips and almost immediately things are misunderstood and/or twisted, often in a way which is negative and undermining to the victim. The obvious effect is that the victim gets a bad name, and those who have heard the gossip have a preconceived idea of what he/she is like, and consequently are on their guard or simply deliberately avoid any contact with them.

The physical and Spiritual effect of such an action is that the 'gossip' receives Reciprocal Action, irrespective of whether he thought the gossiping would do any harm or not. Hence, he pays for the *end* product and attracts a 'glup' of negativity from the Lower Etheric onto his already contaminated aura. Like attracts like - and other similar gossiping and/or back stabbing entities in the Lower Etheric and physical (like minded people) are attracted to this 'glup', affecting and blending with the individual, making it harder for him/her to stop gossiping. The result is, whether the individual consciously realises it or not, that their Inner Density sinks and his Spirit Spark/soul becomes increasingly clouded with negativity until such discrepancy is redeemed.

'But I say unto you, that resist not evil: but whosoever shall smite thee on thy right cheek, turn to him the other also.' Matthew 5 vs 39. Redemption can only happen through 'forgiveness' and only the injured party can forgive another. To forgive with love means that we can free the other person from receiving some or all of the Reciprocal Action or negative trauma, provided they are receptive (or the Reciprocal Action will be a great deal harder). To sum up, only a man who can be silent when it is necessary can be master of himself. As gossips attract gossips, smokers attract smokers, drinkers attract drinkers, like attracts like:- 'But I say unto you, That every idle word that men shall speak, they shall give account thereof in the day of judgement. For by thy words thou shalt be justified, and by thy words thou shalt be condemned.' Matthew 12 vs 36, 37. (The 'day of judgement' here refers to our personal judgement at the end of this current life).

3. RELIGION

The *foundations* of True Religion can be found amongst all Doctrines, but there isn't any one which universally Preaches the *whole truth*. There are some which give false emphasis, distort passages, or even preach outright lies. However, there are also isolated pockets of Truth to be found within any religion, but this is only in cases where the Vicar, Priest or whoever is preaching, has searched hard and worked out the Truth from the Bible, Koran and other such Holy texts, and backed this up with personal experiences and awareness. Their message will not always tally with the doctrines as laid down by the 'Authorities' (particularly the more 'rigid' aspects), but their churches, chapels and other such places of worship, will be bursting at the seams. This is because people, guided by their Intuitive Perception, will naturally gravitate to the Light/ Truth. But, on the other side of the coin, there are churches bursting at the seams where Priests are preaching what the congregations want to hear, which is not necessarily what they need to hear. As Christ said:- 'Yea, and why even of yourselves judge ye not what is right.' Luke 12 vs 57, i.e. at the end of the day we must all work it out for ourselves and not be afraid to question.

There is a lot of hot air puffed out in the various circles of Beliefs, but one thing most religions have in common is 'love thy neighbour as thyself'; that is, 'what is hurtful to yourself do not do to your fellow man.' Provided we stick by this, then surely it doesn't matter how we view or interpret God. This is because God is Love and if we Love all and sundry, then we will be living and working in alignment with God's Will.

'Judge not, that ye be not Judged. For with what judgement ye judge, ye shall be judged: and *with what measure ye mete, it shall be measured to you again.*' Matthew 7 vs 1 -2. This is a perfect example of the Law of Return. This includes judging another's religious views, because if they live by the Word of God and His universal laws, it does not matter whether they are Hindu, Buddhist, or totally unreligious. Judging another's way to be wrong or even misguided, has been the biggest cause of wars over the centuries, and the Reciprocal Action ('it shall be measured to you again') is devastating to those fanatics involved, resulting in their Inner Density becoming very black. 'For all they that take the sword shall perish with the sword.' Matthew 26 vs 52.

'Every kingdom divided against itself is brought to desolation; and every city or house divided against itself shall not stand:' Matthew 12 vs 25. An obsession with any specific aspects of a faith can make us narrow minded and Judgmental, thereby preventing the full picture of God's Will from entering. Look at the distaste between some Jews, whose concepts are based on the Old Testament, and some Christians, whose emphasis is based on the New Testament. There are some within the Christian Church who believe that those who do not follow Christianity will be condemned, even those who are 'unfortunate' enough never to have heard of Christ. Moreover, some people even believe that those within another or different Christian doctrine to theirs, will automatically be cast into Hell's fire; along with all the Buddhists, Hindus and so on. There are, of course, those within the Islamic, Jewish, Hindu and Buddhist religions who are equally Judgmental.

How many times in situations such as these have 'masters',

'doctrines', 'cults', or supposed 'living Gods' placed Kalashnikovs and weapons in the hands of their followers and told them to 'kill in the name of God'. The 'common ground' of 'love thy neighbour', is thereby instantly shattered:- 'They shall put you out of the synagogues: yea, the time cometh, that whosoever killeth you will think that he doeth God Service. And these things will they do unto you, because they have not known the Father, nor me.' John 16 vs 2, 3. Some fanatics feel that their way is so right and others is so wrong, that they escape judgement but;- 'Of judgement, because the prince of this world is judged.' John 16 vs 11 - every last one of us meets the Judgement, and; - 'Yea also the heart of the sons of men is full of evil, and madness is in their heart while they live, and after that they go to the dead.' Ecclesiastics 9 vs 3. If we do allow our dark sides to totally and mercilessly rule our hearts and actions, then there is only one fate and outcome for us on the Day of Judgement - that of Spiritual Death.

Are not the problems resulting from the obsession with the Immaculate Conception another example of narrow-minded religious fervour? Could not such determined emphasis upon the Virgin Birth be partly responsible for sex being frowned upon by many factions as dirty and wicked, pushing it further underground and giving rise to yet more carnal lust, decadence and prostitution? The clue could lie in the meaning of the word Virgin at the time that the Gospels were written, i.e. does it mean a woman who has never had sex, or a woman who hasn't borne children?

According to the laws, is it not possible that Joseph and Mary could have had 'sex' and it was Christ's 'Spirit' that ascended, without his body? Some religious circles are now openly discussing such possibilities. But at the end of the day who cares? Does our rigid doctrine and public debate on these issues and others, such as women priests, impress the general public and encourage them to fill the churches to try and find God in their lives? Moreover, does God, who loves us all equally, care about such seemingly petty and egotistical displays? Or is the grin on Lucifer's face getting yet broader?

What gives any of us the right to judge, particularly when Jesus always directed his words and deeds to God, stating that it was his *word* that is important, *not he* himself:- 'And whosoever speaketh a word against the Son of Man, it shall be forgiven unto men, but whosoever speaketh against the Holy Ghost, it shall not be forgiven him, neither in this world, neither in the world to come.' Matthew 12 v 32. Likewise:- 'If I do not the works of my Father, believe me not. But if I do, though ye believe not me, believe the works.' John 10 vs 37-38.

Bearing in mind the above, Jesus' words:- 'I am the way, the truth, and the life: no man cometh unto the Father but by me.' John 14 vs 6, literally means that everyone who does not follow Jesus himself will be Damned. This would mean that Jesus was an arrogant, judgmental hypocrite. However, it is this point which some 'Christians' believe to be the Truth, that enrages members of Islam, the Jews and Hindus, who feel that Christianity sees itself as superior to all other religions. Likewise, there are those in other religions who feel the same about their Prophets, such as Mohammed. Does not aloofness prevent us from experiencing the One, Universal Religion - that of *unconditional love and humility*?

There is a belief in some circles that when Jesus said 'The only way to the Father is by me', he quite literally means it in terms of a one hundred per cent submission to and embodiment of the 'Christ Energy' as he had done at his Baptism, as being our sole means to salvation. However, such circles feel that

Mohammed, Buddha and other such enlightened beings have also embraced and embodied the Christ Energy, *but* just called it something else, in the same way as Christians worship God, Islamics - Allah and so on. Many feel that they are worshipping a different God in the same way as they feel that their particular human master embodies a different energy to the masters in other religions. Most of us feel that there is only the one God, so in the same way why not just the one energy of God which we humans can embrace - currently called many different names, yet enough to make some fanatics kill over? Jesus continually stressed that the Christ energy was available to anybody who wanted it. Therefore, God sent His Son Jesus to Israel for the benefit of the Western World, His Son Mohammed to Arabia for those in the Middle East, and His Son Buddha for those in the Far East, and no doubt many more. Why not send just one Son for the whole of mankind and save all the squabbling and suffering resulting from what seem conflicting religions? God sees mans hearts. Having given man Free Will and He then gave us just one Book of Truth, it would just take one Emperor or King at any point in history to tamper with God's Book, for his own earthly power and control over the masses, to distort God's Truth for many generations. For example, many today currently feel that all references to reincarnation were removed from the Bible around 500 AD. The idea for this being that if the masses believe they only have one life, they will be more easy to control.

There are some born-again Christians, Buddhists, Hindus, priests, missionaries and followers of all kinds of religions who attempt to convert us to their beliefs, insisting that they have found the only true way to God and eternal life. Again, if this were the case it would be well nigh impossible to state that God is a God of Love. It is therefore vital we understand that there are many ways up the same mountain. For these reasons, evaluating the practises chosen by others is little more than an attempt to do God's work, arrogant and therefore Karmically damaging to our own Spirit. Hence, if we decide to follow a religion/practice, it's up to each of us to choose one that feels true to our heart. It is important to remember that practises are only *vehicles* for us to develop a state of loving - kindness and compassion on the path toward Freedom.

The Parable of the Good Samaritan, Luke 10 vs 30 - 37 emphasises that in God's eyes we are all the same and that we will meet the same Judgement. The Samaritans were condemned by the Pharisees, yet they could 'love their neighbour' reaping the corresponding Reciprocal Action the same as anybody else. Hence, we must constantly be aware of interpreting the Bible consistently in literal terms. Citing Luke 14 vs 26:- 'If any man come to me, and *hate* not his father, and mother, and wife, and children, and brethren, and sisters, yea, and his own life also, he cannot be my disciple.' If we lived according to this creed literally, we would surely turn into monsters?

The Bible is itself full of contradictions should we interpret it all literally. It is a book written by man, divinely inspired or otherwise, and who knows how it may have been slightly altered over the centuries or what's been lost in translations. This is both a blessing and a shame, but at the same time is in accordance with God's Will - see Numerology Exercise earlier.

The quote above - Luke 14 vs 26, demonstrates how literal interpretation markedly increases the number of contradictions thrown up by the Bible. Naturally, if Christ had really used the word '*hate*' here, we would all be pretty shocked. The underlying point of loving God over and above all our family, relations and friends put together is clear enough, but, as we've all experienced, man-made errors do occur - the Bible is a translation!

There are clear cut examples of contradictions when the Bible is read literally. For example, Leviticus 14 speaks of ritual cleansing that a Priest would perform, which is not dissimilar from rituals practised by those who are involved in witchcraft or voodoo. 'And he shall kill the lamb of the trespass offering, and the priest shall take some of the blood of the trespass offering, and put it upon the tip of the right ear of him that is to be cleansed, and upon the thumb of his right hand, and upon the great toe of his right foot.' Leviticus 14 vs 25. Such methods are condemned in other parts of the Bible:- 'To what purpose is the multitude of your sacrifices unto me? saith the Lord: I am full of the burnt offerings of rams, and the fat of fed beasts; and I delight not in the blood of bullocks, or of lambs, or of he goats.' Isaiah 1 vs 11.

Regarding the Old and New Testaments, where do we draw the line, what with so many apparent contradictions between the two books? The Old Testament has some very important Truths which still apply today. However, it was written for the benefit of mankind and his evolution in the world at that stage. The world has evolved substantially since then and hence the need for the New Testament, based on Christ's message.

Christ was always keen to point out he wasn't there to undo the word of the Old Testament but to fulfil it. This meant, according to many lines of modern thinking, that Christ took the old concepts and simply 'updated' them. For example, in Exodus 21 vs 24 it states; 'an eye for an eye, a tooth for a tooth, hand for hand, foot for foot', which may have served a purpose in Moses' day to possibly make people think twice before amputating all a person's limbs for stealing a rabbit. It could be construed that Christ simply expanded upon this concept to help lift mankind on to the next rung of the 'evolutionary' ladder:- 'You have heard it hath been said an eye for an eye and a tooth for a tooth: But I say unto you, That ye resist not evil; but whosoever shall smite thee on thy right cheek, turn to him the other also. Ye have heard that it hath been said, Thou shalt love thy neighbour and hate thine enemy; But I say unto you, Love your enemies, bless them that curse you, do good to them that hate you, and pray for them that despitefully use you and persecute you; That ye may be the children of your father which is in heaven.' Matthew 5 vs 38, 39,43 - 45.

The word 'updating' could be somewhat flattering, since very simply much of the New Testament suggests a complete reversal in many of the old teachings. To take the above quote in Matthew, Christ is quite literally saying the opposite to the 'old' message. The New Testament message of, 'Turning the other cheek, Love your enemies, and not judging/condemning others on any count (discussed in chapter on Judgement)', couldn't be much further removed from Old Testament messages such as:- '…And they shall say unto the elders of his city, This our son is stubborn and rebellious, he will not obey our voice; he is a glutton, and a drunkard. And all the men of his city shall stone him with stones, that he die: so shalt thou put evil away from among you.' Deuteronomy 21 vs 20, 21.

The answer to the question of where do we draw the line between the Old and New Testament, is straight down the middle! This is not to say we should discard the Old Testament altogether, but need to take care in the way we decipher Truth from half Truths to the totally outdated 'truths' - discussed in Footnote. '…Neither do men put new wine into old bottles : else the bottles break, and the wine runneth out, and the bottles perish : but they put new wine into new bottles, and both are preserved.' Matthew 9 vs 17.

The point is that people have used texts from the Bible, the Koran and other religious texts to justify their horrific deeds. In so doing they are fundamentally misguided because the Bible is open to false or distorted interpretation. The Bible provides solace for a great many people and guides us Spiritually throughout our lives. It should not be regarded as a blueprint, because if it is, people can use it as a means to vindicate their actions irrespective of whether they are good or bad. Hence, our only sure way is to find out for ourselves from our own experiences, listen to our hearts and gain as clear a picture as possible from all the religious doctrines and simply by being alive and aware in every moment, so we are not distracted.

It is easy to become confused and even distracted, should we take everything we read literally and try to make sense out of all the contradictions. Relying solely on our intellect will not give us all the answers. When confusion sets in, our ego will often become distorted. For example, one such man, who became quite heavily distracted by his 'Past Lives', went up to a teacher and quite seriously and excitedly said that he had been a Pharaoh in a past life. The teacher suggested he go back to Egypt to claim his inheritance, and:- 'If the prison cell you end up in is anything like the Pyramids, you'll have plenty of time for contemplation.'

It is very damaging to focus on past lives, and in particular assume that we were once one of the more grandiose characters, or focus on who we will be in the future, whether it be an Angel, Ascended Master or some similar Spiritual being. Furthermore, it is irrelevant to our current Spiritual development, and demonstrates a lack of humility. Once we realise that the greatest gift which can be bestowed upon any man is to be in active service to God and carry out His work in every moment of our day, we will be *truly alive*. This simply means the manner in which we conduct ourselves in dealing with whatever situation (particularly the trickier ones) as regards our thoughts, words and deeds.

A disquieting prediction by Christ suggests how far self-deception can go in religious practices. 'Many will say to me in that day, Lord, Lord, have we not prophesied in thy name? And in thy name have cast out devils? And in thy name have done many wonderful works? And then I will profess unto them, I never knew you: depart from me; ye that work iniquity.' Matthew 7 vs 22 - 23. "I never knew you"; these professionally religious types had never allowed God, as Peter allowed Him, to know them with the deep, penetrating love that would have stripped them of falsehood and re-created them in grace.

'And though I have the gift of prophecy, and understand all mysteries, and all knowledge; and though I have all faith, so that I could remove mountains, and have not love, I am nothing.' 1 Corinthians 13 vs 2. When modern day institutional Christianity adheres too rigidly to certain rules taken from the bible, and the ministers feel superior in observing the failure of others, hardened and soured towards other beliefs, and make an idol of their success in 'apparently' keeping 'the Law', then *love* will be absent. Like the older variety of Pharisaism, this is idolatry. Those who are afflicted with Pharisaism are not easily shamed into throwing away their idols, as others might be who make an idol of money or sex.

Likewise, we might become lazy at the apparently daunting prospect of sorting out the truth from the half truths and contradictions, then just sit back and latch on to one or two of the fundamental concepts. However, these too can become distorted unless we continually work hard at increasing our knowledge and strengthening our foundations. For example, when travelling on buses in certain far away parts of the globe, we may encounter drivers who tear round hair pin bends on two wheels, down mountain passes which have no barriers and which boast a host of rusted, crumpled old buses at the bottom of the cliffs. Should we, heart in mouth, point out these wreckages to the driver, in the vain hope he might slow down a little, we'll often get the reply:- 'It's Karma man!'

To sum up, confusion leads to such states as laziness, egotistical behaviour, arrogance, a need to 'control' and the condemnation of other's ways and religious views should they not tie in with our own. Confusion ultimately leads to fanaticism, open hostility and sometimes murder and this is directly opposite to God's message of Humility and Unconditional Love.

As mentioned, there are many paths to enlightenment and selfless love:- 'In my father's house are many mansions.' John 14 vs 2. (This also refers to 'the levels'). These paths are manifest through learning from our day to day tests, or overcoming obstacles by imposing various disciplines upon ourselves. For example, monks learn the lessons through strict self-imposed disciplines, such as abstinence from sex in deed, word and *thought* (the hardest one), and spending much of the day in silence to allow the Christ Energy or Inner Voice to enter in and fill their beings.

The speed of progress to selfless love is, of course, totally down to the individual. How quickly we come to terms with forgiving others for their false judgements, or how long it takes a monk or yogi to be master of his own thoughts to the extent that he is able to banish all sexual fantasy from his mind, depends on the person himself.

Silly thoughts, and thoughts of temptation will always enter into our heads until the day we die. For example, Christ in the Garden of Gethsemane when tired and run down voiced his thoughts:- 'If it be possible, let this cup pass from me,' Matthew 26 vs 39. Moments later he retracted this statement, as discussed earlier, and realigned himself with God. The point is should we dwell on impure thoughts, then our Spirit will be directly affected and the result will be a further build up of our Karmic baggage. This build up is relative to the amount of energy we give such thoughts.

In *all* religions (and people who choose not to follow any particular doctrine), there are those who are aligned with God's Will/the Holy Spirit, and through the hard slog of their individual lessons have separated the wheat from the chaff. Likewise, there will be people who are not aligned and will use religion to service their own ego, as is the case in any other occupation or hobby. When certain cults or sects suck troubled individuals into their beliefs and rituals, is this not the same principle as some religious practices who desire to 'convert' people to their form of worship, whilst judging other forms of religion to be misguided and/or even evil? The Law of Equilibrium is very apparent here, whereby factions within the Christian religion (as in any other), soon fade into oblivion without the necessary *financial and numerical support.*

The use of 'Fear' is often one of the main Tools used by certain cults and some communities and factions within the main Religions of the world. Once an individual's weaknesses are discovered they can be exploited, either to convert them to actively worship solely in the ways of the particular doctrine, or to bring them into line when their Faith in the doctrine is floundering and they are 'asking too many questions', for example. The threat of banishment and rejection from the religious 'family' (and thus God!) normally brings people back into line. This is provided they haven't gone 'too far', and gained too much inner knowledge, light and peace (where fear is exposed, dealt with and then dies), and realised that God will not love them any the less for standing firm on their own in His Light and Truth.

It is vital for anyone who desires to join a Religious or Spiritual Group that they enter into it with their eyes wide open and are not afraid to question anything. This is not always easy because we may be run down, weak and confused at the time. Personal responsibility, however, still applies and provided we keep an open mind the warning signs will be clear. For example, the Doctrine or teaching may gradually encourage us to sever the relationships we have with our families and friends and enter into the 'safety' of their Spiritual/Religious 'family'. We may also be encouraged to delegate certain responsibilities we have in life or even leave them altogether, such as jobs, hobbies and so forth. All such techniques, and many more besides, are the means by which some cults, groups or churches attempt to control, possess and indoctrinate people into their 'Godless' practice. Are the underlying principles of a 'Holy' man who condemns the packed congregation on Christmas Day, or whatever religious festival, of indolence; 'where are you lot for the rest of the year ...?' any different to the 'persuasive' techniques used by certain cults? Do they not both 'desire' to help the souls of others? (with a little financial gain for the particular doctrine, and increase in power from increase in numbers of followers).

How easy it is to slip (more often than not unconsciously), into the trappings and Luciferian failings of certain aspects of religion - namely the need to convert, which often involves the judging of others. Likewise, when the desire to maintain the often spectacular places of worship - churches, temples, mosques and such like is greater than the desire to help people to find God in their lives. Does this not in certain cases, focus the attention of the masses on the earthly power of the church at the expense of the power of God?

Churches provide many with a great deal of comfort and a special time to focus on God. However, the search for God is a twenty four hour a day job and if we forget about the things we've absorbed in between services and feel that God is only really found in churches, then distortions will result. As in all things a balance can be found, but we only have to open our eyes slightly to see how 'balanced' our system is today. As God is *omnipresent*, surely then the only place to find true religion is by looking into our own hearts and conscience with boldness, honesty and integrity? Is not the church the people rather than the buildings?

The Kingdom of Heaven is available to all of us, yet it can't be found by gazing around the sky and stars, but from looking within, sweeping out the rubbish, and then experiencing and allowing the Holy Spirit to fill in the spaces which are left. It is so perfect that no religion preaches the whole Truth - i.e. there is no one hundred per cent correct 'doctrine' - since then we have no choice but to find out *for ourselves*, and in so doing reap the full Karmic benefit.

'The teaching is of the path and the place - seeing is the work of each soul for itself.' Platinus. 'Yea, and why even of yourselves judge ye not what is right?' Luke 12, vs 57.

FOOTNOTE: Why do I use quotes from the Bible to back up my convictions? Some of the dangers of interpreting everything in the Bible literally have been pointed out in this Chapter. We can all of us see the rifts in mankind caused by literal interpretations of pieces such as, 'no man cometh unto the father but by me', and the general confusion resulting from the many apparent contradictions we come across when reading the Bible. It is for these reasons that Christ delivered much of his message in the form of Parables. Also parables encourage us to 'work' ourselves in deciphering the message, and the same is true for most of the Bible due to the way in which it is written.

'For my flesh is meat indeed, and my blood is drink indeed. He that eateth my flesh, and drinketh my blood, dwelleth in me, and I in him. This is that bread which came down from heaven: not as your fathers did eat manna, and are dead: he that eateth of this bread shall live forever.' John 6 vs 55, 56 and 58. Theologians, Intellectuals and Politicians spent 1000 years arguing about whether or not the actual body and blood of Christ was present in the bread and wine at Christian Communion. God's Truth is very simple and something we feel in our *hearts* which we can then express, interpret and put into words using our heads. But, it doesn't matter how much of the 'Holy Spirit' is in the bread and wine or floating around us, we will never feel it if our hearts are not open.

Lucifer is very subtle - should our hearts be closed and we rely solely on our 'intellect' to solve various issues and arguments, we will never understand God's simple Truths. This is because our pampered ego may run riot as we strive to 'prove our case', with all the ramifications as our base emotions come to the fore, when not everybody agrees with us. Also, as mentioned, is the humble man in the street impressed by such 'intellectual' discussions, when he can see so many people suffering and needing help in his community, and does it make him want to go to church as a result? 'Let no man deceive himself. If any man among you seemeth to be wise in this world, let him become a fool, that he may be wise. For the wisdom of this world is foolishness with God. For it is written, He taketh the wise in their own craftiness. And again, the Lord knoweth the thoughts of the wise, that they are vain. Therefore let no man glory in men. For all things are yours.'

1 Corinthians 3 vs 18 - 21.

Therefore, the more we can feel the Bible in our hearts as we read it, the more we will understand and 'see' whether a passage or verse is meant literally or symbolically. A couple of simple examples are:- 'Jesus saith unto them, my *meat* is to do the will of him that sent me, and to finish his work.' John 4 vs 34, and:- 'Labour not for the *meat* which perisheth, but for that meat which endureth unto everlasting life.' John 6 vs 27. Clearly Christ is not referring to the meat on our dinner plates here.

Barnabas 10 (from the Codex Siniaticus) writes an excellent piece about the symbolic meaning behind the references to 'food' in the Old Testament. In Deuteronomy 14 it states:- 'Thou shalt not eat any abominable thing,' verse 3 and verse 8, 'And the swine, because it divideth the hoof, yet cheweth not the cud, it is unclean unto you: ye shall not eat of their flesh, nor touch their dead carcass.' Barnabas interprets the symbolic meaning behind the various animals mentioned. He states that it is not right to be like or consort with men who are like swine. That is to say, when they have plenty they forget the Lord, just as the swine when it eats does not know its Master, but when it is hungry it cries out, and after receiving food is again silent. It is impossible to interpret such pieces of the Bible literally because if God meant us not to eat meat, for example, man would have been created a Herbivorous Ruminator.

There is no one hundred per cent clear cut reference to reincarnation and the Ethereal body in the Bible (that I have found!), but we do get indications, depending on how we interpret the passages. For example, there is a 'hint' at reincarnation in Mark 9 vs 11 - 13:- 'Why say the scribes that Elias must first come? And he answered and told them, Elias verily cometh first, and restoreth all things; and how it is written of the Son of Man, that he must suffer many things, and be set at nought. But I say unto you, That Elias is indeed come, and they have done unto him whatsoever they listed, as it is written of him.' Likewise, a 'possible' reference is made by the Angel Gabriel when talking of the coming of John the Baptist:- 'And he shall go before him in the Spirit and the power of Elias, to turn the hearts of the fathers to the children, and the disobedient to the wisdom of the just; to make ready a people prepared for the Lord.' Luke 1 vs 17. However, the point is that do we believe that God is a God of Love, because if we do and we see our fellow man being born into lives of starvation, disease and death at a very young age, and we believe we have only one life/one chance to reach Heaven, then what is our definition of Love, when such children don't even have the chance to get started?

1 Corinthians 15 verses 40 and 44 state respectively:- 'There are also celestial bodies, and bodies terrestrial: but the glory of the celestial is one, and the glory of the terrestrial is another.' and:- 'It is sown a natural body; it is raised a Spiritual Body. There is a natural body, and there is a Spiritual body.' There is no mention of an Ethereal body. However, it was mentioned earlier that it is due to our 'Ethereal' body that our Spirit gravitates to its correct level in the Ethereal realm to have the lessons appropriate for it. If it was 'raised a Spiritual Body' after one lifetime of 'good behaviour', and therefore goes to Heaven, then again suffering (particularly of young children) on earth becomes utterly pointless and we'd be seriously struggling to stand up and say that God is a God of Love. The meaning of 'it is sown a natural body' in the context of this book means that we remain in a 'body' which corresponds to our level of lightness and needs until we are one hundred per cent pure when we can be raised a Spiritual Body and go to Heaven.

It is possible to see how interpreting everything we read in the Bible literally, using solely our intellect, i.e. the analytical, scientific mind, could be enough to drive some people mad! The Truth is in the Bible, but we need to search for it with our *hearts* first and foremost. It will also help to be open minded enough to study and learn from other religions - Oriental religions are full of endless references to reincarnation. As when reading any book, we can 'feel' what is Truth and what is not, should we listen to our hearts backed up by our daily experiences. If we are not broad minded, then we will never know the reasons why things happen as they do.

4. THE POWER AND THE GLORY AND RESPONSIBILITY

It is quite incredible how we underestimate the Perfection of God, and the fact that He is the 'Power and the Glory', in that He is all powerful, knowing and present in every living thing. We all too frequently impose our Will over His, with the audacity to think we know what's best. Our knowledge in comparison to God's is less than that in our little toe nail compared to the total knowledge in the whole Solar System.

We even try to 'tempt' him, as the Pharisees did to Jesus when asking him for a sign and Jesus said:- 'An evil and adulterous generation seeketh after a sign: and there shall no sign be given to it, but the sign of the Prophet Jonas.' Matthew 12 vs 39. Any obvious sign would be depriving us of relieving our Karmic Burden and is indicative of our indolence that we can't be bothered to realise and take on board the concept:- 'Straight is the gate, and narrow is the way, which leadeth unto life, and few there be that find it.' Matthew 7 vs 14. When our eyes are open we will see 'miracles' in every moment of the day.

'Thou shalt love the Lord thy God with all thy heart, and with all thy soul, and with all thy mind. This is the first and great commandment. And the second is like unto it, Thou shalt love thy neighbour as thyself.' Matthew 22 vs 37 - 39. First we need to find out what is God's Will, which we can only do on our own. Books and manuscripts are only pointers - there is no substitute for experience. Hence, much soul searching, hard work and honesty is required, but:- 'Ask and it shall be given you: seek, and ye shall find; knock and it shall be opened unto you.' Matthew 7 vs 7. This means sow with the right attitude and you will reap.

SINCERE PRAYER WORKS (see *Footnote*), particularly if we end it, 'but let *thy will* prevail always', and have complete faith that whatever the outcome, it will be the best for the Spiritual Growth of all concerned - even though this may not be in accordance with our will or other people's. 'But when ye pray use not vain repetitions as the heathen do: for they think they shall be heard for their much speaking. Be not ye therefore like unto them: for your *father knoweth what things ye have need of, before ye ask him.*' Matthew 6 vs 7 - 8. Hence, all we really need to say in prayer is - 'Thy will be done', or pray along the lines of asking to be given the strength to accept what is in God's plan for us. But to seek reassurance about 'progress' in prayer would be to reinforce the ego's desire for security.

By saying, 'Thy will be done', as opposed to, 'let My Will be done', and if this results in damage to our bodies or the stripping away of 'unnecessaries' we may be very attached to, then be willing to accept this. So when something happens in our lives which shatters our security, such Reciprocal Action is due to God's love and Will (No Blade of Grass ...). This means that our Spirit has attracted this situation to give us the opportunity to off-load more of our Karmic baggage.

It really is worth waking up and taking note of the warnings and lessons we're given, because the Judgement, in accordance with God's Will, is *inflexible*:- 'Every tree that bringeth not forth good fruit is hewn down, and cast into the fire.' Matthew 7 vs 19. This principle is repeatedly rammed home in the Old

Testament, such as the perdition of Cain and the parting of the Red Sea for Moses and the Children of Israel, and the subsequent death of those in pursuit. Who knows when the 'Global Judgement' of mankind is due?

God is *love* and loves the world, which he proved by sending down his Son. Jesus' life was very much an example of how we should lead our lives and if we fall short then we will reap the corresponding Reciprocal Action affecting our Inner Density. When Christ said on the cross: 'Forgive them, for they know not what they do;' he is referring to the fact that *we murdered the Son of God.* Pilate succumbed to the overriding will of the masses, who opted for a complete rejection of Christ's message - Law Of Equilibrium. Christ did 'die for us', but only to show us how far removed we are from God's Truth and to show us how much God loves us despite this, giving an idea to those who strive for it, of how much work needs to be done. For example, Christ by forgiving all those who condemned him even though he was an 'innocent man', sets the sort of standard God demands of us if we are to enter Heaven. This is what is meant by Christ being 'The Way'.

'And they were judged every man according to their works.' Revelations 20 vs 13. This is one of many references to the fact that we will be held responsible for the consequences of *all* our actions, thoughts and words - we reap what we sow. Hence, to pile all our sins upon Jesus is an excuse by many of us *not* to take full responsibility for our every action, thought, word and deed, and hence, in so far as the global 'equilibrium' is concerned, demonstrates how man chooses Mammon before God - a Testimony to the 'apparent' mess the world is in today. God is Forgiveness, but His forgiveness is based on our endeavour to forgive others - The Law of Return (see footnote on Forgiveness at the end of the book).

We only have to look around the countryside on a beautiful
Spring day to see the immaculate beauty of God's creation -
the hymn 'All things Bright and Beautiful', describes it
perfectly. Many artists have been inspired and played a major
part in opening people's eyes to the beauty of our surroundings
and in the preservation of the countryside. However, no artist
can get anywhere near capturing the perfection of what we
can see around us, such as the sun lighting up the new gold/
auburn leaves of a Copper Beech, the light green canopy of
young leaves on a massive Oak, the carpet of bluebells on a
forest floor and the billions of new audacious sunsets. (a) A
painting stays the same: and (b) The colours on a canvas are
nowhere near as vivid or pure as the real thing.

Yet, it is man's way to spend millions on some painting - often
just bolstering the pockets of a few middlemen (the original
artist may have passed on): Yet, with such vast sums of money
he could have bought an area of wasteland, planted an
assortment of trees of his choice and gained inward pleasure
at nurturing and watching such a place of beauty develop,
change and mature.

In this case, the pleasure gained is in the giving of something
to the world, without a lot of song and dance; whereas the
ownership of a valuable painting, in addition to the inner
pleasure the piece gives, can bolster the ego of the owner
(should he allow), due to the adulation and/or envy of others.
The same principle naturally applies to all our possessions,
whether they are of value or not. Hence, we constantly need
to ask ourselves:- Are the outward pleasures of our actions,
possessions, words and so on, in alignment with the lightening
of our Inner Density? And to what extent are we truly giving
of ourselves? 'For where your treasure is, there will be your
heart also.' Matthew 6 vs 21.

FOOTNOTE: 'Ye ask, and receive not, because ye ask amiss, that ye may consume it upon your lusts.' James 4 vs 3. All too often prayer is based on self-interest of the most blatantly egotistical kind, which unashamedly refers to material gain rather than Spiritual benefit. Also, some of us expect God to direct our lives in every detail, with no regard for our own personal responsibilities in respect to behaviour and decision making. Expectations of God to do this or that can lead to an attitude of undue familiarity and a devaluation of His true status. Through such presumptuous prayer, we will attract the necessary situations into our lives so as to help us to get back on line. For example, something may well happen along the lines of what we've prayed for, but we might get the feeling of 'this is not what I had in mind'. Therefore, we may dislike what we see and it may result in a huge knock to our ego. Our immediate tendency may be to get angry with God for not doing 'precisely what we asked of Him'. However, another alternative and sometimes the only one in instances when we've been knocked hard enough, is to humble ourselves before him in reverential awe instead of over-friendly palliness.

Hence, when we pray for help in dealing with a situation, the 'help' may come in the form of circumstances 'being created' to give rise to an unavoidable confrontation with another or the group of people with whom we have the problem. This may not be what we had in mind when making the prayer, but should we deal with it correctly (see Chapter on Fear), and not run away from it, we will find the answer to our prayer - which again is probably not what we originally expected. When we say, 'give us this day our daily bread', we are not just praying for our physical bread, but also our 'Spiritual bread'; i.e. our daily lessons, trials and tribulations which give us the opportunities that are best suited for our individual Spiritual

Growth.

In order to grow, we must give to others. Prayer is a form of giving, and the more that we humbly and sincerely pray with love for others, and in particular our enemies, then the more we can be a 'servant of God' like Peter was. The Prayer of St Francis of Assisi sums this up. 'Lord, make me an instrument of your peace. Where there is hatred, let me sow love ...... O Divine Master, grant that I may not so much seek to be consoled, as to console; to be understood, as to understand; to be loved, as to love. For it is in pardoning that we are pardoned; it is in dying ... that we are born to eternal life.'

5. JUDGEMENT

'And why beholdest thou the mote that is in thy brother's eye, but considerest not the beam that is in thine own eye? Or how wilt thou say to thy brother, Let me pull out the mote out of thine eye; and, behold, a beam is in thine own eye? Thou hypocrite, first cast out the beam out of thine own eye and then shalt thou see clearly to cast out the mote out of thy brother's eye.' Matthew 7 vs 3 - 5.

Judgement means making a decision when we say, do or even just feel something, having weighed up a person, people or situation. 'Speak not evil one of another, brethren. He that speaketh evil of his brother, and judgeth his brother, speaketh evil of the law, and judgeth the law: but if thou judge the law, thou art not a doer of the law, but a judge. There is one lawgiver, who is able to save and to destroy: who art thou that judgest another?' James 4 vs 11, 12. Should we make a decision to say or do something, because we feel another is wrong, misguided or even evil and we condemn them, in however small a way, (for example should they ignore our opinion), then we are *judging them*. This is God's job not ours.

However, if we give our opinion/observation/judgement and they still do completely the opposite and we feel nothing but sincere love for the individual and wish them 'all the best', then we have *not* judged *them*. This is because we realise that only God can judge and should they decide to go down a particular path which we feel is going to be harmful, it could in fact be beneficial because this person may need the experience (which appears negative and a mistake on the surface) to assist them in their Spiritual Growth, should they learn from it. This is discussed more fully in the Chapter on Suffering. Therefore, our emotions of love or those of anger, bitterness, jealously, disappointment and so on tell us whether or not we have 'judged' (condemned) another.

'For though I made you sorry with a letter, I do not repent, though I did repent: for I perceive that the same epistle hath made you sorry, though it were but for a season. Now I rejoice, not that ye were made sorry, but that ye sorrowed to repentance: for ye were made sorry after a godly manner, that ye might receive damage by us in nothing. For godly sorrow worketh repentance to salvation not to be repented of: but the sorrow of the world worketh Death. Wherefore, though I wrote unto you, I did it not for his cause that had done the wrong, nor for his cause that suffered wrong, but that our care for you in the sight of God might appear unto you.' 2 Corinthians 7 vs 8 - 12 (excluding vs 11). This is what is meant by, 'casting out the beam out of thine own eye'. Therefore, there is a distinction between passing a Judgement with sincere compassion and unconditional love for another, and judging them with any other emotion inside us, which means that we are not leaving the judgement *of them* to God. In the case of the latter we directly damage ourselves and further darken and bind our Spirits; 'but the sorrow of the world worketh Death'.

For most of us, judgement is a killer. It is something we should be aware of and work on in our daily lives, by being conscious of how wearing down and painful it is to not only the recipient of our judgement but also ourselves. The more self-justified we 'feel' we are, and the bigger the bee in our bonnet, the more we grind ourselves down, which can affect our own physical health if allowed to continue unchecked. Any 'Judgement' of another is in effect our desire for them to think and behave as we do.

Even the most Holy and Righteous people are susceptible to the many pitfalls concerning daily Judgements whilst on earth. Particularly when dealing with those closest to us, our love can subtly change and become conditional and obsessive (discussed in Chapter on the Family), because we find it more and more difficult to forgive if they're not doing what we want them to do. Our values go out of the window in these situations. As in all things, we have attracted such circumstances to give ourselves another opportunity to grow, and depending upon how we react, it is God's way of showing us that we still have a long way to go before we embody the energy of God - that of unconditional Love and Humility. In this state we will be free from any desire to control, influence or manipulate another. 'But them that are without God judgeth. Therefore put away from yourselves that wicked person.' 1 Corinthians 5 vs 13. The more we 'judge', the less we love and the more we squeeze the light of God from our hearts.

One of the best features of the Spiritual/New Age Path is the *emotional clearing aspect* - working on our deep blockages to flush them out. This work has limitations, because there is no substitute for the experience our daily lessons give us to help show us our weak points, on which we can work on if we so choose. Also, if we don't continually work on such 'clearing' in our daily lives, there will be little benefit in doing Emotional clearing therapy and workshops. This is similar to going to Church every Sunday, and then forgetting about the things for which we've prayed during the weekdays. However, at least it gets us on the right track of trying to make ourselves better people.

The overall idea is that if we are in a mess ourselves, how can we help sort out the mess in others? This gives such Spiritual work the label of 'selfish' by many, but Jesus said:- 'Thou blind Pharisee, cleanse first that which is within the cup and platter, that the outside of them may be clean also.' Matthew 23 vs 26. A clean exterior is useless hypocrisy without a pure interior. Hence, 'Never judge a book by its cover'.

Once we've done some Emotional clearing and removed many of our blockages, then those we thank and love the most are those who've come into our lives and given us the most potent and often heart-rending confrontations with our own weaknesses and short-comings. From these, if we are sincere, we learn the true values of forgiveness, patience and humility, which will hasten our Spiritual Growth towards the light. It is then that the perfection of every aspect of God's Creation expands within us and we simply stop worrying in the knowledge that all is as it should be ... *now*.

We all of us wear different masks based on our emotional and mental states, and these masks frequently change as we go through life. When we feel anger, jealousy or envy, due to the behaviour of another, it will help to detach from the emotions that are flying around and ask, 'why have I attracted this situation into my life?' It also helps to remember that behind the mask before us, there is a light body and a pure Spirit Spark.

Hence, we're not being asked to condone what another does or does not do, but we can choose to love and admire the orb of light emanating from the Spirit Spark in everyone, and have compassion when a fellow being has allowed dark emotional shadows to cloud their Spirit. Only the most courageous people with real *faith* will be able to discard all their masks and allow their inner light to shine through unhindered. This is the hardest thing we can do, because we will be totally exposed and vulnerable in this state - discussed in chapter on Faith. The late Sir George Trevelyan made a conscious decision in 1987 to never speak or think a bad word or thought about anybody else. Frail as his body was, the love and power emanating from this man was awesome.

Compassion and understanding for another who succumbs to the very strong temptations of the earth is vital, because we *all* of us have succumbed to temptation to a greater or lesser degree. Also, it is easy to forget that we attract someone with a 'specific mask' into our lives to give us a specific challenge and the opportunity to grow. Therefore, should we 'hate' another, we are judging them, further binding our own Spirit and in no way helping to change our surroundings for the better. 'If a man say, I love God, and hateth his brother, he is a liar: for he that loveth not his brother whom he hath seen, how can he love God whom he hath not seen?' 1 John 4 vs 20.

Christ certainly appeared not to like the masks of judgmental arrogance and superiority worn by the Pharisees. However, in his love for them, Christ did his utmost to reduce the thickness of the Pharisees' masks by pointing out the 'right way'. It must be remembered that Christ had removed the 'beam and mote' from his own eye before judging the ways of others - how many of us can say the same?

'Let brotherly love continue. Be not forgetful to entertain strangers: for thereby some have entertained angels unawares.' Hebrews 13 vs 1 - 2. How can we feel superior (Spiritually or otherwise) to another? For example, there is a story of Christ knocking on the door of a 'good man' one morning and asking if he could come to dinner that evening. The 'good man', who has become 'good' because he gives to the poor and always helps those in need, excitedly prepares a feast fit for a King. Whilst he's waiting for Christ, an old lady arrives seeking shelter from the rain. The 'good man' gently explains that any night other than the current one would be fine because he's expecting Christ for dinner at any moment, and turns her away. Next, a beggar knocks on his door asking for some food and is turned away for the same reason. The 'good man' then waited up all night but Christ never showed up. A week later Christ returned to the 'good man's' house, who was none too happy and asked where he'd been whilst showing him all the food that had gone to waste. Christ then pointed out that he did come and asked if he recalled the old lady and the beggar who turned up.

Likewise, the drunk tramp on the pavement, that we many of us have crossed the road so as to avoid any potential contact, could be an 'Angel' who has 'given' of himself to bring to the attention of many of us our haughtiness, aloofness and hence lack of humility, on which we can then make a change if we so choose. It is possible that an individual is a 'mature soul' who just needs one more earthly life wearing a particularly thick mask, so as to give him the opportunity to shed his last piece of Karma, before he enters Heaven. For example, the lesson might be greed, whereby the Spirit is born into a society of selfishness, which is wholly 'Mammon' orientated and where everyone is determined to make more money than their neighbours - at any cost! We may look at such a person and feel Spiritually superior, because we don't have the fanatical attachment to money that he does. However, we may be a much younger soul and are not ready for this test yet, and we may need a few Millennia of Karmic lessons and tests before we are.

But, when the 'Mammon man' in this case wakes up to the values of money in alignment with God's Will and not man's ('waking up' may either happen progressively or suddenly, in that the whole lot is stripped away), he will no longer be greedy and/or selfish and will go straight to Heaven when he dies as a mature Spirit -provided he hasn't picked up any new Karma. Again, how can any of us judge another, because an individual's Spiritual Development and Karmic lessons are between them and God. 'Judge not thy neighbour until thou art in his place' - we may have similar experiences to others but, how can we ever know how another feels about their experiences, particularly since there are often many lessons going on at any one time. Also, our current tests are all to some extent influenced by our past experiences.

There are many Doctrines that quite rightly encourage the philosophy of looking and going 'within' and 'listening to our hearts' before acting accordingly. This is because there is often a vast difference between God's Will, which we find in the core of our heart, where our Spirit Spark abides and which gives out pure Unconditional Love; and Our Will - which is often focused, to a greater or lesser extent, on our own personal needs and desires. In the case of the latter, selfishness often dominates. The clue as to which way we gravitate being given by the degree we display the base emotions or those of love. When we are selfish, we look solely to our own needs, and these feelings are intensified by our ego which encourages us to look 'outside' of ourselves for what we think we need, and for the reasons why things aren't working in our lives. This equals Judgement which can lead to *blame*.

In condemning others, we directly condemn ourselves and thereby eliminate light from our bodies and love from our hearts. Therefore the more we condemn and judge, no matter how self-justified we may feel or whether we are *right* or wrong, the worse we feel in ourselves. As we become more run down, our immune system and hence resistance to disease weakens.

When we condemn another verbally or mentally, we are displaying a base emotion. As with any base emotion, this is directly showing us something we need to look at in ourselves, as discussed throughout this book. Also, as mentioned, due to the Law of Attraction, our focus and the resulting type of emotion gives us an accurate indication as to the aspect of our personality which needs addressing and sorting out. This has massive implications. Whether it be something we hear about or are ourselves directly involved - in condemning another/others we are being shown that there is a similar energy/potential within us. In this light it means we most of us have the potential to be a murderer, rapist, child abuser and such like. With the 'correct' circumstances and continued pressure on the 'right' button we have it in us to commit the most horrendous atrocities. For example, what if we were born into a society where murder and rape were socially accepted or if there was a complete and utter breakdown in our current society and anarchy ruled? Would we be able to hold to our moral principles if the pendulum of Equilibrium swung almost completely to darkness, where many people were getting their main kicks from rape, murder and abuse? 'If you can't beat 'em join 'em!'

We may well feel that we could never kill another under any circumstances. However, war is commonplace in many countries throughout the world and anarchy rules in parts of these countries. Imagine it was us in the position of those suffering and how we would feel if our fellow man/men destroyed our homes, and killed and raped members of our family. Would our focus be on compassion and forgiveness, or bitterness, hatred and revenge - and could we not possibly inflict something similar on our 'enemy', should the opportunity present itself to us?

Do we think we can embrace God and His Love in our hearts, whilst we hold feelings such as revenge deep within our beings? There are many within different cultures, creeds and race throughout the world who still focus negatively on the suffering inflicted upon their ancestors. When we feel the need for revenge as opposed to compassion, understanding and forgiveness, how can we embody and live a religious life?

Therefore, condemnation is simply wasted energy and damaging to our Spirit, since by our thoughts and actions *we judge ourselves* - in the same way as when we die physically - 'As above so below'. For example, should a group of handicapped people go into a public swimming pool and the 'normal' people get out, the latter thereby judge themselves - nobody else has to say or do anything, since any such person will feel the shame gnawing into their hearts. Likewise, 'For if there come into your assembly a man with a gold ring, in goodly apparel, and there come in also a poor man in vile raiment; And ye have respect to him that weareth the gay clothing, and say unto him, Sit thou here in a good place; and say to the poor, Stand thou there, or sit under my footstool: Are ye not then partial in yourselves, and are become judges of evil thoughts?' James 2 vs 2 - 4.

Judging ourselves is healthy work, but the judging of others which is often centred around our desire for them to think as we do, leads us further away from the light of God. It is often when our 'Desires' - secret to us or otherwise, are frustrated, that we are displeased and shaken and may find ourselves pointing a finger at others. Hence, *every emotion outside a state of grace* is telling us *'we're not there yet!'* Diversity of opinions, doctrine or creed between fellow men, countries and holy men can give rise to such emotions. For example, the 'Judgement' of certain 'established' religious custom towards Tarot, crystals and such like - given the blanket label of *'evil'* - and the Judgement of certain mediums or clairvoyants, who may look down on the church with distaste as mundane and dogmatic. What gives those priests a right to judge the practice of another, and those who contact 'Spirits' the right to judge themselves superior to those who cannot? 'For my thoughts are not your thoughts, neither are your ways my ways, saith the Lord.' Isaiah 55 vs 8. If God were the sole object of our heart's desire, would we be bothered by the erring fancy of our Judgement or Belief Structure?

'Woe unto you, Pharisees! for ye love the uppermost seats in the synagogues, and greetings in the markets.' Luke 11 vs 43. This is one of many scathing attacks on the ego of man whether it be ostentatious praying, 'look what a holy man am I, clad in a garment of purity', and/or casting our alms, whatever they may be, before men saying 'look at me'. Even the Son of God referred his all to God, so all that is not *performed in humility is performed in vanity*, with the corresponding Reciprocal Action. It is amazing how most of us can't see the glaring faults within ourselves and then won't do anything about them even when we do get a glimpse - other than allow our 'masks' to thicken yet further. To sum up:- If Jesus Christ came to Earth today, do you think he'd be treated any differently by the respective powers that be, than he was 2000 years ago? More to the point, can any of us say that we can see clearly enough to recognise him if he did come today?

6. SELF-RIGHTEOUSNESS

'If I justify myself, mine own mouth shall condemn me: if I say, I am perfect, it shall also prove me perverse.' Job 9 vs 20. Self-righteousness and justification is one of the biggest pitfalls most of us slip into. The underlying principle is contained in the Parable of the Pharisee and the Publican, Luke 18 vs 1 - 17:- 'And he spake this Parable unto certain which trusted in themselves that they were righteous, and despised others:' The attitude of the Pharisee being - 'I thank thee, that I am not as other men are .... I fast twice in the week, I give tithes of all that I possess.' The attitude of the publican:- '..would not lift up so much as his eyes unto heaven, but smote upon his breast, saying, God be merciful to me a sinner.' God's attitude:- 'For every one that exalteth himself shall be abased: and he that humbleth himself shall be exalted.'

We demonstrate our self-righteousness in a multitude of ways. For example, some vegetarians can be damning of those who 'devour little innocent lambs, thereby fuelling further animal hostility'. 'Not that which goeth into the mouth defileth a man; but that which cometh out of the mouth, this defileth a man.' Matthew 15 vs 11. Could there not sometimes be a craving for a double cheeseburger in such situations? There is nothing wrong with the discipline of vegetarianism or fasting, provided we don't start thinking we're more certain of going to Heaven than others:- 'Ye judge after the flesh; I judge no man.' John 8 vs 15. An inevitable consequence of any self-righteousness is the Judgement, again, of others, *but*:- 'He

that is without sin among you, let him cast the first stone.'
John 8 vs 7.

Have we ever heard the Dali Lama, who perhaps has a more
'earthly' right to be self-righteous and judge others than most
people, say a word against the Chinese who are suppressing
and inflicting terrible suffering upon his Tibetan people? The
reason is not that he is scared of being murdered - physical
death being merely a stepping-stone to greater work - but the
knowledge that through such suffering many people are
working off the necessary Karmic Debts in their incarnation
and circumstances. This is not to say that we should go rushing
off looking for problems and suffering - our Spirit will always
provide us with exactly what we need. 'For the work of a
man shall he render unto him, and cause every man to find
according to his ways.' Job 34 vs 11. The Dali Lama, as with
any reasonably good person, will naturally bleed with
compassion at the suffering being incurred by his people, do
what he can to lessen their pain and no doubt wish we could
all live in peace and harmony. But, he doesn't have to look far
back in history for the reasons why; which combined with his
understanding of God's Karmic Laws, means that he will be
able to view the situation in a different way to most of us.

Each individual will 'reap what they sow'. 'For the Lord seeth
not as man seeth; for man looketh on the outward appearance,
but the Lord looketh on the heart.' I Samuel 16 vs 7, and:-
'but God knoweth your hearts; for that which is highly
esteemed among men, is Abomination in the sight of God.'
Luke 16 vs 15. Is not self-righteousness thus little more than
Snobbery - Spiritual or otherwise, with the corresponding effect
on our Inner Density?

7. HUMILITY

Humility is putting ourselves last, least and lowest. Vanity is the opposite - putting ourselves first, most or highest. 'Let no man deceive himself. If any man among you seemeth to be wise in this world, let him become a fool, that he may be wise. For the wisdom of this world is foolishness with God. For it is written, he taketh the wise in their own craftiness. And again, the Lord knoweth the thoughts of the wise, that they are vain.' 1 Corinthians 3 vs 18 - 20.

Grace can only enter the humble. It is very good for us to be wrongly judged by man when we're doing our best - how often do we let pride take control when our plumage is ruffled, even if someone accuses us of the minutest falsehood:- 'The beginning of all temptations to evil is instability of temper and lack of trust in God.' It is far easier to work on 'an eye for an eye' than to 'turn the other cheek'. Hence, humility is the only way to overcome this vicious circle:- 'Whosoever therefore shall humble himself as this little child, the same is the greatest in the Kingdom of Heaven.' Matthew 18 vs 4.

This is not to say that we should become doormats but if we stand in God's Truth, we will be persecuted (discussed in chapter on Faith):- 'But beware of men: for they will deliver you up to the councils, and they will scourge you in their synagogues: And ye shall be brought before Governors and Kings for my sake.' Matthew 10 vs 17, 18. Today's society is, generally speaking, centred upon man's current attitudes of greed, selfishness, envy, pride and so on, and most of us don't like it when it is pointed out that by giving in to such temptations, we are forcing ourselves further away from God instead of drawing closer. 'It is not what you gain but what you give, that shows the worth of the life you live.'

When others are bearing rash or false judgements upon us and our faith is firm, we are able to bear their accusations with humility and understanding. In such situations, there can be nothing more annoying for the 'Judge', because he feels all his words and emotions reflected straight back, and the more he continues the more he hurts himself -provided we don't capitulate to his level. But if we are seething beneath a cool exterior, we also have a long way to go, and need to beware of suppressing emotions which will create deep blockages in time if not faced up to.

As in all things, when we're being wrongly 'judged', we must acknowledge that we have attracted this situation for our development. Should we react with anger and try to convince and even pressurise our oppressor into realising and apologising for their misjudgement, our base emotions come to the fore. 'For the wrath of man worketh not the righteousness of God.' James 1 vs 20. Moreover, by stoking the fire, the fire gets bigger and the one making the judgement feels more and more self-justified, which results in *their* becoming less humble with the corresponding increase in Inner Density.

If they do admit their error, we may feel pleased in a way, but often it leaves a deep feeling of dissatisfaction and hollowness at the whole incident, relative to the degree of hurt and strain at the time. Hence, if we're 'honest' we will feel regret and an inner wish that the whole thing had never happened, because our feelings of satisfaction at the conclusion will be far outweighed by the pain caused by the dominance of our base emotions during the incident.

The alternative is to speak our mind calmly and with understanding for the one making the judgement, and allow the knee jerk reaction to become angry to simply wash over us. *Faith* in God and His Will is a huge help in such situations, but even if we have no faith, we can always choose to walk away if we wish, in the knowledge that our own conscience is clear. Yet, if we can project back love to our 'Judge', he or she is far more likely to look into his/herself and maybe make some fundamental changes for the better. Whether they acknowledge this or not to us is irrelevant, since it is only our 'ego' which desires acknowledgement/apology. If our accuser does apologise to us even grudgingly, beware of smugness. Accept his/her apology gracefully and treat the incident like it never happened. Again, Unconditional Love to all mankind (*humility*), is the key to helping make the world a better place, and at the same time lightening our own Inner Densities.

We most of us want to be a 'somebody', respected by others for our achievements and abilities in whatever field our desires and energies lie (inclusive of the 'street cred' gained from hooliganism and crime). The more importance we attach to this, the greater become our fears of being just plain old Joe Bloggs/Mr Average. God knows whether we are working and living to the best of our abilities or not, and the extent to which we are giving of ourselves or are being selfish and greedy, and who else's opinion of us really matters? Most of the significant Biblical characters were from ordinary 'Joe Bloggs' origins. For example, Isaiah, Daniel, John the Baptist and Jesus, who was himself a carpenter's son.

Even the most famous and successful Kings such as David humbled themselves before God and their people, for whom they were, in effect, a servant. Likewise, King Arthur built the Round Table to encourage everybody, particularly himself, to be humble before each other and therefore God. However, once the egocentric bravado of some of the knights took hold the regime was bound for collapse, even though the original intentions had been good. The greater our material wealth and social deification, the harder it is to be humble - as discussed in the chapter on Mammon. King Solomon for all his wisdom turned to other Gods and Goddesses at one point in his life, under the wily influences of some of his many wives and concubines, who were not believers in the one God.

The more we are touched by the praise and flattery of others, the more puffed-up and vain we tend to become, and conversely, the more vulnerable we are to condemnation - equal and opposite. Many of us feel a little 'praise' (not to be confused with 'encouragement'), does us good and gives us a boost. However, total humility means dedicating *all* our good deeds to God, so any praise we receive from others will encourage us to become more and ever more humble, lest our egos get the better of us and lead us to pride. The less influenced we are by the opinions and praises of our fellow man, the more room for God-consciousness we make within us, provided we humbly dedicate our all to God. 'It is better to trust in the Lord than to put confidence in man.' Psalm 118 vs 8.

'In as much as ye have done it unto one of the least of these my brethren, ye have done it unto me.' Matthew 25 vs 40. This means that we are being asked to do to others as we would do to Christ or God - how we give to others, behave and conduct ourselves before them and so on. It also means what we don't do for 'the least' we don't do for God. For example, when somebody is driving us mad can we remain tolerant and patient? And when we are being wrongly judged, can we face our accuser without malice and treat them as Christ or God testing our love and forgiveness?

When we find ourselves with somebody over whom we have always felt a bit 'superior', and they register our arrogance, then there will be no communication of any significance. Should we find the strength to humble ourselves a little before this person and get off our high horse, we may well end up having a very interesting conversation and actually gaining something ourselves. For example, when sitting with someone who is twittering away, we tend to feel exasperated, bored and want to be elsewhere with somebody else. In other words we feel superior to this person. The more they 'sense' our arrogance, the more nervous and inferior they feel and end up twittering all the more on increasingly mundane subjects. By projecting such arrogance, it doesn't make another shut up any quicker - in fact it is normally quite the opposite due to the fear of complete humiliation our acquaintance feels at departing from someone who is so utterly bored and fed up with their company. When they leave we may have such feelings as 'thank heavens they have gone, what a tiresome waste of time that was, now I can get back to what's important!' What we probably do not realise is the feelings of humiliation and lacking that the other person feels - whether consciously or subconsciously. Therefore, we are responsible for them twittering or whatever all the more the next time they find themselves in a similar situation. This, combined with fuelling our own feelings of superiority, doesn't help to lighten our Karmic burden and Inner Density - 'Whatsoever you do to the least of my brethren ...' By humbling ourselves enough to show our vulnerable side to such people, we may well be amazed at the depth within them and the extent they give to us and we learn from them.

116

Every moment of every day we have lessons and opportunities to grow and develop. The more aware we are about ourselves and how we are dealing with even the minutest thing, the more we will see how we keep getting similar opportunities until we master our response in a positive way. With awareness we will clearly see our progress as our negative responses modify and subside, and feel a blast of euphoria within our being when we cope with the particular lesson with understanding, love and forgiveness. It is in such times as these when we will get a deep inner knowing that we will never have to have that lesson again as we move on to the next rung. This is provided we don't 'slip back' - in which case we will realise we have deceived ourself in that we had not fully mastered the particular situation/lesson. This is the Spiritual life at work on earth.

Some people find the need to travel the world to 'find themselves' which is healthy if the individual feels that this is his/her best way forward. However, it doesn't mean that they will necessarily have more opportunities than those who stay at home for financial reasons and general commitments. It is our responses to every situation, person and challenge in every second of our lives that is important and dictates the speed that we 'find ourselves'. The more our 'awareness' develops, the more we will notice the numerous little coincidences, chance meetings and so on in our daily lives which never cease to amaze. However, how easy it is to lose sight of all this when confronted with an obstacle we find hard to bear. Yet, if we can muster the strength to remember the above in our darkest periods, by detaching for sometimes just the briefest moment, and realise that like the good things then the apparently not so good things are there to help us in some way also, we will find it easier to find the light at the end of the tunnel.

This means that we must be aware of our thoughts, actions

and words in every moment, checking and acknowledging when we 'slip', and say or think something negative about someone when they perhaps irritate or disappoint us. We should, of course, humbly thank such people for bringing such a weakness to our attention, until such time that we can *be* beings of light and love, twenty four hours a day. It's a bit like driving a car. When we're learning we need to look at and check all that we touch - gear lever, pedals and such like, until it becomes instinctive.

In an 'enlightened' state we will touch all those with whom we come into contact, and we will be truly 'giving' of ourselves. Only then can we be a true servant to God (See *Footnote*). How often, in those moments, when we're in a state of love walking down a street do many people smile at us, even when we're not smiling ourselves and feel we look no different to normal? Conversely, how often do people cross the road when we're dragging our emotional burdens/hurt along with us?

Humility and love increase as the Perfection of God's Creation dawns on us. 'Blessed are the meek: for they shall inherit the Earth.' Matthew 5 vs 5. Is any judgement of another's practice/ beliefs included in the definition of humility? To be humble is to see everybody in the world as 'enlightened' except yourself.

THE BEAUTY OF DEATH: This is a time of enforced humility, even for the most arrogant, conceited person. Regardless of what possessions we might have and what others might be saying - for good or ill, all our old ego-centric masks are stripped away at this time, because the focus is on 'what's next?'

The less attachment we have to the transient 'things of the earth', such as materialism and, as far as other people are concerned, emotional and mental attachments, expectations, the need to control and so on, and the more humble we are, then the less we will fear physical Death. 'The sting of death is sin; and the strength of sin is the law.' 1 Corinthians 15 vs 56. At Death we have absolutely no control at all as to where we'll end up next, since this is governed by God's Universal Laws. Hence, the more we are the type who needs to control and/or manipulate people and situations to fulfil our personal needs and desires, the more agonising will be our experience of Death - 'the *sting* of death is sin'.

FOOTNOTE: Exactly how an individual is 'touched' by an enlightened one very much depends on their state at the time. Most of us will gain a reflection of our Inner selves - pure light/love acts as a mirror, making us aware of our guilt, resentment and shame, at the emotional baggage we are carrying around with us, or immense comfort and joy, or most frequently a mixture of both (and many other emotions).

Whatever the reaction, an Enlightened person performs an act of 'Unconditional Love' by standing firm in 'Truth', in that we can see ourselves for what we really are by our response to such people, and are thereby given the opportunity to work on ourselves if we so choose. However, many of us in our indolence become angry, judgmental and even aggressive when we don't like what we see. The best example of this is Christ, who always caused a reaction whether of love or hate or a mixture of the two. 'True Humility is not submission to human authority, but total disregard of it when reality speaks to us.' John Oman.

8. WORK

We are very much on this world to work, in whatever form that may take. 'But wilt thou know, O vain man, that faith without works is dead? Was not Abraham our father justified by works, when he had offered Isaac his son upon the altar? Seest thou how faith wrought with his works, and by works was faith made perfect?' James 2 vs 20 - 22. It is through work that we can best work off our Karmic chains, and hence our greatest fear should be that of stagnation which induces regression if allowed to continue. How often do people die within months of retirement, because their Spirit feels that if the person is going to sit back and learn no more lessons, it may as well move to the next 'place' to continue its work towards the light. 'By much slothfulness the building decayeth; and through idleness of the hands the house droppeth through.' Ecclesiastes 10 vs 18.

P. Ouspensky, and other such philosophers, very much stressed the work ethic, but in contrast to the modern day 'competitive' education system advocated the importance of each individual doing the work to the best of their ability *in their own time*. This is because Spiritually, Physically and Intellectually, we all progress at a different pace. Many of us have experienced that if we rush through the basics, and hence don't have good foundations, everything else is meaningless - Maths at school being a common example for many of us.

The Parable of 'work', Matthew 25, 14 - 30, involves God

giving one man five talents, one two and another one. At the day of reckoning, the first two had both made another five and two talents respectively, and both were rewarded the same, because both had left the world a better place than when they arrived. For our Spirit it doesn't matter what we've got or do in this sense, because everything is relative, provided we do our best with the gifts given to us - material or otherwise. But the man who was given one talent, and buried it for the period for reasons of lack of courage, fear and laziness, was seriously rebuked by God:- 'Thou wicked and slothful servant ...' because he came back with exactly what he was given to work with. Therefore, he made no profit and did nothing with his talent.

'I am the true vine, and my father is the husbandman. Every branch in me that beareth not fruit he taketh away; and every branch that beareth fruit, he purgeth it, that it may bring forth more fruit.' John 15 vs 1, 2. How many times have we heard it said, 'I've been giving all my life, now it's my turn to sit back and receive'. True happiness only really comes when we are in *active service*. For example, a boss is in service to his workers as much as the other way round, in order to keep the company afloat so that everybody can earn a living. The more aligned we are, the more work and thus responsibility we are 'given' (in the same way as our Spirit attracts bigger and bigger tests the more we move to the light, discussed further in the Chapter on 'Fear').

It is only by giving unconditionally of ourselves through work and all other aspects of our life (see Footnote), and expecting nothing in return, that we truly grow Spiritually. Any 'expectations' to the contrary are stifling, conditional and binding to our Spirit:- 'For if ye love them which love you, what thank have ye? for sinners also love those that love them. And if ye do good to them which do good to you, what thank have ye? for sinners also do even the same. And if ye lend to them of whom ye hope to receive, what thank have ye? for sinners also lend to sinners, to receive as much again.' Luke 6 vs 32 - 34.

'But this I say, He which soweth sparingly shall reap also sparingly; and he which soweth bountifully shall reap also bountifully. Every man according as he purposeth in his heart, so let him give; not grudgingly, or of necessity: *For God loveth a cheerful giver.*' 2 Corinthians 9 vs 6, 7. Not only does the Law of Returns operate 'to the letter' regarding our giving, but our Spiritual rewards are also relative to the joy with which we give and whether we can keep the genuine smile on our face even when we're doing the most unpleasant or seemingly dullest of work.

Because it is in through giving that we receive, it is vital we allow others to give to us, if they want to, provided they are giving with genuine love. How often do many of us feel guilty at simply receiving, when there are no strings attached, and/or spend the time looking for a catch - which is again a reflection on the state of our world.

If we block the giving of others, we are in fact directly blocking their Spiritual Development, and due to our guilt and fear of being 'indebted', we are committing a selfish act and thereby degrading their love. Just imagine if everybody felt guilty about receiving, then none of us would be able to give and 'grow' anyway! Christ naturally enjoyed having his head anointed and massaged by a lady at, 'the house of Simon the Leper', Mark 14 vs 3-9, and his pleasure at receiving gave extra pleasure and joy to the lady anointing him. There is, of course, a huge difference in receiving with complacency (the 'takers' of this world), and with gratitude, love and pleasure.

In the Parable of the Hired Labourers, Matthew 20 vs 1-17, the 'Householder' of the vineyard hires men at different times of the day, and at the end of the day pays them all the same. It is important that when we're working and have agreed a payment not to become preoccupied with that which others are receiving, since our resultant Base Emotions will directly harm our Spirit. Again, is it not more important to, 'lay up our treasures in Heaven?' We may have worked more than our payment, but never mind, because God knows, and any complaining directly drags us down and away from God, and how will we ever be 'chosen' whilst we have any trace of bitterness or resentment towards the lot of others? 'Is it not lawful for me to do what I will with mine own? Is thine eye evil, because I am good? So the last shall be first, and the first last: for many be called, but few chosen.' Matthew 20 vs 15, 16. No blade of Grass ... It will help to remember that there are *no coincidences* when receiving what we may feel to be a 'pittance', relative to that which we feel we deserve. We should calmly detach ourselves from the situation, and ask ourselves, 'what is this lesson here to teach me?'

In the Parable of the Pharisees and the Publicans, Matthew 21 vs 28-31, a father asked his two sons to go and work in his vineyard. The first said he would not go but then did (the Harlots and the Publicans), and the second that he would go but then didn't (the Pharisees). 'Verily I say unto you, That the publicans and the harlots go into the Kingdom of God before you.' Matthew 21 vs 31. This again reiterates the need to work quietly and with humility, as opposed to with self-righteousness and any feeling of aloofness. Should we enjoy the adoration and respect of others, we're not even at the level of Harlots in God's eyes; 'so the last shall be first, and the first last'. It must be stressed that the above concept of 'work' not only applies to our daily jobs but *every* situation in our lives, such as how we communicate with and treat others from our workmates to family and friends, shopkeepers, tramps and so on.

FOOTNOTE - on Giving. If there is a 'need' God will guide us. Therefore, if we by God's Grace are given an opportunity to help another or others, take it for we will be serving God by doing so. No matter how small or large the opportunity, we ideally should not pass it by if we can help. Therefore, help that old lady across the street; give money or food or clothing to the poor and needy; be a comforter to those who mourn or are sad; be strong for those who are flagging. Whatever it is, be it humble or great, do it if you have the means and power to do so. And even if you yourself do not have the means to help directly, seek out others who do, for you are still helping even if you only form the link between the one in need, and the one who can give. Therefore be not prideful and try to do what you cannot do, for you may make things worse, and neither be too afraid or timid because you can't help and so pass on by.

9. KIDDING OURSELVES

We humans are brilliant at convincing ourselves that we're purer than we actually are, and maybe than the next man too. If we're reading a Book of Truth, like the Bible, and we're reading a piece we feel to be too much for us to take on board, and which would require a major upheaval in our lives, we have the ability to completely 'block' such passages, allowing them to flow straight over us until we come to a gentler bit which we can relate to, and which enables us to see ourselves in a 'Godly light'. The pieces we tend to block out most are those which encourage us to look within, face up to our deep desires, emotions and attitudes and make the corresponding changes in our personality to align with God's Will. These could be pretty drastic!

We only have to remember the times when we think that we have the total Truth of any given matter and judged another as a result, only to find other pieces of the 'picture' reaching us afterwards which tell us otherwise. We many of us still find it easy to kid ourselves even in this situation, by latching on to one or two aspects (true or not) and shutting our ears and eyes to the rest.

Likewise, regarding those times when we think we are ready for something yet we are still too immature or in need of more work. This is a common occurrence in many aspects of life - particularly for those who are endeavouring to live a more 'Spiritual' life. As mentioned earlier, a medium (for example) may be progressing steadily and laying down a firm foundation, but then due to a tinge of boredom or ego, feel 'prematurely' that they have their foundation and can now reach out to contact the 'Higher Beings'. Without a firm grounding in Love, Humility and Forgiveness, we will be chicken fodder for entities in the Lower Etheric. They simply fuel our weak spots, which is normally our ego and a desire for some excitement, by encouraging us to feel that we are contacting the Spirit of God, Jesus, Archangel Michael and so on. The 'motives' of these entities are discussed in the chapter on Lucifer. But, it is in this situation when we think we are climbing the Spiritual Ladder, that we are actually sliding down it. Again, even if we then end up confused and aggressive to those who don't believe in us, we can manage to kid ourselves that we are better off and lighter than before we embarked on this path. However, we must remember that God is Forgiveness and always waiting patiently for us. Should we humbly and sincerely admit our folly once we have recognised it, then repent, His arms will be open and we will have learnt a valuable lesson regarding, in this example, our ego and impatience. This same principle applies to almost all aspects of our daily life, such as work, relationships and past-times.

In general, one of the great fears we have is that of change, but if we didn't need to change, we wouldn't have to be here, because we would have already attained purity and entered the true 'Spiritual Realm'. Hence, if we refuse to change, there's little point in this earthly life. To take the expression 'A leopard never changes its spots' - this is simply not true. Should we feel that this is true, because we are too old or set in our ways or it is 'simply not the done thing', then we are kidding ourselves. The consequences of this sort of stubborn self-deception are indolence and stagnation. Conversely, we can kid ourselves that we have changed when in fact we haven't or have only gone part way. However, the more we constantly strive to be aware and open to all things that life throws at us and humbly listen to the lesson that each experience gives us, we will be in a better position to apprehend Truth. Some of the most glossed over 'Truths' are 'love thy neighbour as thyself', and 'judge not that ye be not judged'.

10. FEAR

Fear is simply a lack of faith. Likewise, *all* our insecurities (being based on fear) reveal a lack of Trust in God. 'And fear not them which kill the body, but are not able to kill the soul: but rather fear him which is able to destroy both soul and body in hell.' Matthew 10 vs 28. To fear God and the consequences of not following His way is healthy and the only thing we really need to fear. This is not to say we should become gibbering wrecks, hence, fear of God is more akin to a reverential respect.

Our greatest fears tend to be those of pain (mental and emotional as well as physical) and death. The more we believe in God and understand the point of our daily lessons, and as our belief in an afterlife increases, the less fear we will have of Death. However, we may still fear dying in pain and continue to fear the idea of pain, such as if we get a serious disease or a severe mugging. For example, a woman walking through a street or park late at night having missed the last bus, will often fear being mugged or raped. This subject is discussed in detail in the last Chapter, however, a knowledge of the way God's Will operates and Faith in God will help tremendously. 'Yea, though I walk through the valley of the shadow of death, I will fear no evil: for thou art with me; thy rod and thy staff they comfort me.' Psalm 23 vs 4. It is the ultimate comfort to know that God is with us at all times, and even should the worst happen that there is a good reason as to why. Remember that there are huge potential karmic benefits (discussed later), and that there are no coincidences. Hence, 'Fear not them which kill the body, but are not able to kill the soul'. No human can touch our Spirit, and the deeper our Faith becomes, the less fear we will have as the more we realise that it is our Spiritual Growth that is all important - our physical body being simply the ideal housing for our Spirit to learn the lessons it needs, via our emotions, thoughts and so on.

Similarly should, if we are one who meditates, have great difficulty in making ourselves able to 'unclutter' our minds from our daily thoughts, concerns and 'things we have to do', then this is indirectly showing us our Lack of Trust in God. This is because we worry that if we totally switch off, we may forget some of the 'important' things we need to get done during our day/week. 'Therefore take no thought, saying, What shall we eat? or, What shall we drink? or, Wherewithal shall we be clothed? (For after all these things do the Gentiles seek:) for your heavenly Father knoweth that ye have need of all these things.' Matthew 6 vs 31, 32. This is the same as when we worry about a situation we need to deal with, and we start to imagine all sorts of negative outcomes.

Any such worries are a demonstration of our insecurities and show us how we are still dependent on our own Will or that of another person's, as opposed to giving up our 'self' to do and trust God's Will. When we have some measure of real faith, we will boldly confront and deal with our every situation with calmness and love, leaving the outcome, whatever it may be, to God. 'But when they deliver you up, take no thought how or what ye shall speak: for it shall be given you in that same hour what ye shall speak.' Matthew 10 vs 19.

The Law of Attraction - should we 'fear' anything of the earth, we will attract and be drawn to the object of our fear, perhaps through other fearful people and beings around us. This is when we tend to start judging the actions of others and so our

Inner Density falls. Equilibrium - the world is living in fear due to the cumulative fearful thoughts amassing in the Lower Etheric, which originated from us, merging with and 'exciting' fearful actions on the Physical Plane (energy generated cannot be destroyed only transmuted - basic physics).

Hence, *fear* can be a hindrance to our Spiritual Development. How often have we experienced a singing or rush from within our being at the idea of doing something or being in a situation more attractive than the one we're in at present? Then, as our mind returns to reality we feel our stomachs tighten and a sickness in the pit, as we reflect on our current environment where we're trapped and bogged down by so many things - such as finances and people. We may then convince ourselves we couldn't carry out our full responsibility to our children or family in any other situation and 'It is clearly not our right or God's Will we should be happy anyway'. Self pity, moroseness, boredom and Spiritual Indolence at life may well creep in, as we know we're not fulfilling our potential and purpose.

But it is Fear of things like the unknown, pain and loss etc., which prevents us from taking any drastic action. We may well go part of the way and end up demonstrating the base emotions to those involved, centred around our frustration. In this situation fear is not of what is happening now, but of what might be; as our imagination whirls, we think and mentally experience the worst possible scenario with close friends and family, or whatever situation.

As in all things personal, everything is relative, because what might be a pebble to one is a boulder to another. Likewise, the Karma worked off is relative, because we are all individuals with different desires, fears and experiences to learn, but, as mentioned, we will never attract a challenge that is too great for us. Hence, let fear be our ally, since it is one of the greatest pointers as to the conviction of our Faith and the extent that we are genuinely learning from our daily 'lessons'. 'There hath no temptation taken you but such as is common to man: but God is faithful, who will not suffer you to be tempted above that ye are able; but will with the temptation also make a way to escape, that ye may be able to bear it.' 1 Corinthians 10 vs 13.

Genuine heartfelt prayer is 'heard'. It is highly recommended to pray and ask God to show us the best way to deal with a problem. We will then get exactly what we need to know - no more and no less, which will normally be an inkling as to what our next step should be. We may well not like what we see. For example, we may fear the consequences in a number of ways, such as the potential for mental, emotional or physical hurt, or the knowing that we must forgive another who has done us an 'unforgivable' wrong. We will probably attract the latter experience when our ego has become inflated and we seriously need to humble ourselves to realign with God, which will necessitate making some fundamental changes in our character. The more aloof, arrogant or proud we are, the harder this will be.

This can be likened to coming across a problem in our lives which seems like a mountain of stones. If we pray sincerely for help, the stones will be laid out before us so we can meet and hopefully overcome the challenges. The mountain will often have developed in the first place when we have repeatedly run away from the tests. Likewise, the story of Jason and the Argonauts from Greek Mythology: When Jason finally managed to locate the Golden Fleece - a symbol of Healing and Enlightenment, similar to the Holy Grail in Arthurian Legend, he found a nine headed Dragon guarding it. Every time he cut off a head another two grew in its place. It was only when he courageously faced up to and plunged his sword into the heart of the Dragon, leaving his fate in the hands of God as he passed by the snarling heads, that he reached the Fleece. There is only ever one solution to any problem!

If we prayed to God to magically remove the 'Dragon' or 'Mountain', and there are many of us who have asked for this, He would be depriving us of the lessons we came down to Earth to learn. God would not desire to remove the boulders anyway, otherwise it would undermine the fabric of His whole, perfect Karmic Creation. If He did, then this proves that it isn't God who has removed our problems but Lucifer, and anyway, Lucifer can only make it 'appear' that the problems are removed, and thereby *delay* the moment we face them and thus *delay* our Spiritual Growth.

Our Spirit is meant to be *free*. If we remain 'bound' in whatever situation for our whole life, we will have to incarnate again and maybe again in a similar situation, no less hard or binding, or deal with it in the Ethereal Realm (excepting when such a lifetime is 'needed' to work off a Karmic debt - discussed in next chapter). This will happen when we continually lash out at the 'heads' or run away and refuse to tackle the core of a problem. Faith in God is, as always, our greatest weapon and protection, since it takes courage to wade into the many snapping heads and get at the heart. It is clear that the sooner we confront our Dragon, the easier we will overcome it, because it will have fewer heads. But, how often do we duck and dive until our backs are pressed so tight to the wall, that we have nowhere else to go or hide and nothing more to lose. We can still overcome the Dragon even then, should we plunge at the heart. As mentioned, the dragon 'outside' is always a reflection of something we need to deal with 'inside'.

However, there is a threshold limit, which varies according to the strength of the individual, where we have continually refused to look at and tackle our problems, when there will be too many heads and we are overcome. We are all familiar with the feeling of knots building in our stomachs, a tightening of our chests and throats and headaches, when there's a problem in our lives we know we need to face. It is through blockages, our Physical, Mental and Emotional states weaken, our energy levels drop and resistance to disease declines.

Similarly, when we are overcome by a problem, it is possible to see why our Spirit might produce disease in our bodies or 'orchestrate' a serious accident, thereby forcing us to face up to and deal with aspects of ourselves. If it is Humility we need for our Spiritual Growth, then should we become crippled we will also have the opportunity (provided we don't become too bitter) to become more humble, as also happens when we get a terminal illness. This is because we will get to spend more time on our own with little to do except reflect on our life, its values and where we went wrong, then hopefully make a *change* for the better. Likewise, a less severe accident or disease may help to slow us down a bit, when we're haring round and round in ever decreasing circles. The concepts in this paragraph may seem cruel and heartless in many ways. However, for all we know our Spirit has been attracting gentler opportunities for hundreds of years to help us to learn a certain lesson and grow, yet for whatever reason, we have opted (Free Will) to turn away or keep our fingers in our ears. This is expanded upon in the last two chapters.

It is only once we have faced up to the problem and the fears that accompany it, and made the necessary changes in ourselves, that we break that particular Karmic cycle and our Spirit is Free to progress to its next set of lessons in accordance with God's Will. Once again it's important to stress we cannot fool God, who knows us better than we know ourselves, 'for man looketh on the outward appearance, but the Lord looketh on the heart.' 1 Samuel 16 vs 7, and His laws are inflexible. For example, when we prepare an imaginative and very 'helpful' crib sheet to get us good marks in a test or exam, we get quite irritated when teacher lectures us on how, 'if we cheat we're only cheating ourselves'. We always get shown up in the end, whether it be in our final exams, when the supervision makes it much harder to cheat, or in the job we get based on our 'inflated' qualifications.

As mentioned, it is the fear of the consequences of striking at the heart of the Dragon that is far worse than actually doing it. The more we can fully come to terms with the fact that whatever challenges come our way are designed to help our Spirit to grow, the better equipped we will be to cope. This may mean that our physical bodies, emotional and mental states suffer. Which do we hold more dear?

11. THE FAMILY

The family provides a very important function in the bringing up of children. The child will naturally be influenced accordingly, whether they be brought up in a loving, secure home or in a den of domestic arguments and violence, alcoholism or drug addiction. We would most of us love all children to be given the best possible start in life. However, the much used phrase, 'we don't choose our parents or relations', rings very true. As mentioned, the family into which we are born is no coincidence and it is the ideal environment for our Spiritual Growth, giving us the best opportunities for clearing our individual Karmic debts. It is very easy to forget that as far as God is concerned, it is our Spirit's Growth and maturation that is important. Our physical and mental states (limited to this lifetime only) are secondary, and are there only to serve as an extension for our Spirit's needs.

It is always important to remember that our children are not really ours but God's, and it is our responsibility to bring them up as best we can in accordance with the Will of God. 'And whosoever shall offend one of these little ones that believe in me, it is better for him that a millstone were hanged about his neck, and he were cast into the sea.' Mark 9 vs 42. The consequences of abusing the 'privilege' of bringing up one of God's children are very serious indeed. For example, being overly possessive to the extent we try to control their every action, thought and word - to be distinguished from giving them a firm telling off when they do wrong. If our desire is to

---

138

possess or control any other person, not just our children, the consequences are the same.

Any binding of the Spirit is not natural, although our trials, tribulations and restrictions are also the means by which the Spirit matures. Sometimes patience and endurance of the problem may be what we need. But, any base emotions resulting from suffocation, expectancy from others and society, are clear signals that there's something we need to deal with. If we had Faith, we would pray and ask for guidance first before acting upon our volition. However, based on the decision we make, we must be prepared to take full responsibility whatever the outcome.

All marriages are made in Heaven. This means those that do work and those which don't, because if a marriage fails all parties involved will receive some fairly major Karma which gives each individuals' Spirit the opportunity to grow and change. Separation usually occurs as a result of the couple becoming dependant upon each other to feel fulfilled, at the expense of God in their lives. Being 'joined together as one' simply results in a power struggle, bitterness, hurt, jealousy and so on, because two individuals with their own desires and path to walk need their own space to express themselves and grow. True love means supporting and loving our partner no matter what they may do. What if they have an 'affair' we may ask? Real love means we will not betray the trust of our partner, no matter in whatever distant part of the globe we may be, nor will we even desire to have an affair.

However, should our partner have an affair even when we are 'clearly in love', then it is *our* reaction that is all important. This will prove a real test of our love, Spiritual maturity and understanding. Should we have the attitude of 'I love you, therefore I own you', then this will result in all the damaging emotions of anger, devastation, regret, fear and even hatred. This is because we interpret love as possession. Real love is so endless and without judgement or condition, that we love a person for what they are, not what we say they must be. In this case we will firstly forgive our partner, then help them selflessly in any way we can. There are many stages between these two reactions, but as things currently stand in the world many of us may feel the latter approach to be impossible and even wrong. However, if we wish to stay with our partner and heal the relationship but there is a part of us which doesn't or 'can't' Trust them, then we have not fully forgiven them. This principle is discussed in detail in the final chapter. If we cannot forgive and trust our partner then there will be an imbalance in the relationship with all the difficulties this brings. We can, of course, only do the best we can in the situations in which we find ourselves. However, our attitudes and emotions in such circumstances will clearly show us where we are at Spiritually in terms of our understanding of love.

'It hath been said, Whosoever shall put away his wife, let him give a writing of divorcement: But I say unto you, That whosoever shall put away his wife, saving for the cause of fornication, causeth her to commit adultery: and whosoever shall marry her that is divorced committeth adultery.' Matthew 5 vs 31, 32. There is, naturally, a very strong argument that getting divorced is a 'cardinal sin', having 'vowed before God' that we would stay with our partner until one or the other dies, and this is correct. However, it must be remembered that the more sincerely we make our vows to God the more he will 'hear' them, as is the case with how sincerely we say a prayer. More significantly, since God is omnipresent i.e. everywhere and in everything *the same*, it doesn't make any difference whether our promise or 'word' to anybody about anything is made in a pub or before the altar. What is important is the sincerity with which we make the promise (a marriage vow is, on the whole, made with the utmost sincerity), and the returning Karma is relative to this, in the same way as should we steal a packet of gum from a supermarket, or break into somebody's house and steal all their personal possessions. The Karmic consequences of committing a sin has been discussed at the end of the section on God's Will, using stealing as an example. 'Thou shalt not steal' is one of the ten commandments the same as, 'Thou shalt not commit adultery', hence, the exact same principles apply if they are broken.

'But I say unto you, That whosoever looketh on a woman to lust after her hath committed adultery with her already in his heart.' Matthew 5 vs 28. We all of us 'sin' in every day of our lives in thought, word and/or deed to some degree. Lust is one of the most common of sins, but far from the only one. Should we, therefore, be imagining somebody else whilst making love to our husband or wife, then we are committing adultery, because in defiling the heart of our spouse, we defile our own heart.

Likewise, if, for example, we lust after and even fantasise about a buxom barmaid. Should we 'listen', we can feel the damage this does to us. When we focus on such thoughts, and we're honest with ourselves, we will not be happy, feel knotted up inside, and any serenity and grace we may have felt before rapidly disappearing. *But* our Karmic load is further increased should the barmaid be affected by our leery glances, thoughts and maybe comments. The more 'sensitive' she is, the more she will pick up on our thoughts and those of our fellow drinkers. This may result in her relating to men more and more on a sexual level. Like attracts like - her relationships may then take on a more carnal basis. As her Spirit becomes increasingly clouded her confidence will fall as she feels the only way she can get affection from men is through her body.

However, her pure Spirit Spark within will be crying out for real love, but as her inner density increases, which will happen relative to the degree the leery, lusty approaches of men affect her and the degree she succumbs to any temptation as a result, then the less her chances will become of finding it. This is because the Law of Attraction means that she will only attract men at a level of density similar to what she feels are her 'needs'. The opportunities for Spiritual growth resulting from this universal Truth are discussed at the end of the last chapter, but the Karmic load of all those involved will be affected.

Lust is a very real energy and, as is the case with all energy, is neutral and can therefore be used positively or negatively. Our Spirit lusts after wholeness and perfect alignment with God. However, depending on our inner state, we can distort this energy and transmute it into earthly lust - whether it be carnal, materialistic or whatever. The emphasis on lots of sex and making as much money as possible, is incessantly rammed down our throats through the media, television, advertising and books. This makes for a very intense testing ground to prove our lust for Spiritual values over and above our materialistic and carnal lust. Earthly lusts are probably the most common of all the 'sins', and as such they are one of the most accurate self-measuring devices available to us as regards our lack of wholeness.

The points surrounding sex and more importantly the consequences resulting from the act, and even thoughts and sexual fantasies, are a very big deal. The more flippant we are and the more our focus is on 'free' love, then the less free we really are as we will be binding ourselves to earthly desires and thereby preventing God's love and light from expanding in our hearts. Abortions, contraception and the killing of so called 'street children' in some parts of the world are a reflection of our flippant attitudes towards sex.

It must be said that the Catholics do have a point regarding their attitudes to sex - abortion, very simply, results in the taking of a life and according to the ten commandments is a cardinal sin, 'Thou shalt not kill'. Therefore, the Karmic consequences on the Inner Density for the individuals involved are very great. These days, it is not uncommon once a woman has had one abortion, to have another and another. The effect this attitude has needs no explanation. Ideally, the way to work off the Karma of pregnancy resulting from a 'casual' affair is to have the baby and both parties to take full responsibility in the bringing up of the child. During this period the attitudes of the couple towards sex will certainly change whether they get on with each other or not. If, due to circumstances, it is impossible for either person to bring up the child, then adoption is certainly the next best thing. In taking responsibility for having the child and finding suitable parents, this will certainly be an attitude-changing, karmically positive solution. In either case the Spirit of the child will have a body and a life, during which it will have opportunities to work off its own karmic baggage.

However, whatever happens it is not the job of the Catholic Church or anybody else to judge or condemn those involved. Mother Teresa, when asked how she felt about homosexuals when the Bible clearly condemns such a practice, replied referring to those with the AIDS virus:- 'We don't judge these people, we don't ask what happened to them and how they got sick, we just see the need and care for them.'

It is through all our actions, thoughts, and so on that we are 'punished or rewarded' according to the Laws of Karma. God is all forgiving, but it is through his laws working automatically (which means we are *all* treated the same), that we can be forgiven whatever the wrongs we have done. To be forgiven we need to a) acknowledge our sin, b) repent of our sin, c) ask for forgiveness and d) be prepared to forgive others. All the Universal Laws of Karma have been designed to help us work towards a state of Spiritual wholeness, no matter how things appear to be on the surface.

Should a marriage break up, the Karma is extra hard because there are so many other people involved, such as close family and friends. However, as is the case with any trial and tribulation, all those involved are given the chance to grow Spiritually - which is down to the individual. If children are involved, it must be remembered that this is very much a destiny point for them , and for whatever reason (between them and God), their Spirit needs this experience for its growth. (Abuse and domestic violence are discussed in the final Chapter of this book).

Kahil Gibran in his book 'The Prophet' says, 'Love each other, but make not a bond of love', and, 'The Oak Tree and the Cypress grow not in each other's shadow'. This is contrary to many marriages of today where people feel 'Bound in Marriage', and where they tend to feel their partner is their possession. This is not Love, Trust or God's Will. However, some people appear to be perfectly happy being answerable for everything to their partner, feeling extra security perhaps but, what about their Spirit?

On the other side of the coin, staying with what we feel to be our surly, grumpy partner for life, could be the paying off of a debt incurred in a past life. For example, in a previous incarnation, we may have given birth to a child who we didn't want and treated it very badly as a result. Hence, to pay off the Karmic Debt, we may give ourselves up to a life in an unhappy relationship to learn the lessons of patience and selfless love. Here again who are we to judge the rights and wrongs of anybody else's situation?

'A mans foes shall be they of his own household.' Matthew 10 vs 36. We tend to be harder in 'judging' our own family and loved ones due to our expectations and inner desire for them to think and adhere to our 'acceptable moral standards/ code of conduct'. In so doing, we directly drag ourselves down through such *conditional loving*.

To take an example of a dog and its master. When the dog has an 'accident' and makes a mess, the master becomes angry and rubs the dog's nose in the mess. Not only does the dog get the mess all over its face, but the smear on the carpet/floor gets bigger and more ingrained and therefore becomes harder to clean up. Also, the master in his fury and lashing out at the dog gets some of the mess on him. This simply makes the master more angry, who then becomes more prone to keep his eye open for any messes the dog makes in the future. The master reacts with the same anger at even the slightest mess/ accident that the dog has.

The dog always tries its best to please its master and get things right because it loves its master unconditionally and always will. However, the harder the dog tries, the more little 'slip ups' it has to the fury of its master. The master becomes so blinkered in wanting his dog to be exactly like him in thought and deed, that he explodes in front of the dog's friends and acquaintances, thereby further humiliating the dog and making it more nervous resulting in yet more 'errors' and so on. Sometimes the dog has his face rubbed in a mess that it can't even see.

The longer this goes on the more the dog realises that it can't be like its master, because it's a different individual. This results in the dog seeking to avoid its master as much as it can, not through lack of love, but so as to avoid the confrontations so confusing, hurtful and draining to both the dog and the master and anybody else in the neighbouring vicinity.

The master thinks it is because of his 'love' for his dog that such actions are necessary. Deep down, of course, the master does truly love his dog. However, it is only as the dog withdraws, no longer seeking its master's praise and even support having experienced time and again how quickly such pleasant emotions change, that the master will have time to contemplate the effects of such conditional love, and his 'need' to control.

It is no wonder that Christ advocates:- 'Verily I say unto you, except ye be converted, and become as little children ye shall not enter into the Kingdom of Heaven. Whosoever therefore shall humble himself as this little child, the same is greatest in the Kingdom of Heaven.' Matthew 18 vs 3, 4. Most adults find it impossible to love *unconditionally*, as a child does. *But*, if we want 'out' of this Karmic cycle, this is the sort of standard we must meet and embrace.

When somebody close to us is trying to control or manipulate us in some way they will run round and round us trying to find a weak spot that can be prised open. They may say many hurtful things, many of which we may feel to be wholly untrue. Naturally, the closer we are to our 'adversary', the better equipped they will be to expose our weaknesses. It will help to remember during such situations, that any aggression from another is always directly related to their own insecurities, fears and hang-ups.

But, it is equally important to know that we have attracted these circumstances to show us something we need to look at within ourselves. For example, should we start justifying ourselves or condemning the other, then we have failed the test in every way. Not only will the hooks of the other penetrate us, but they will feel justified and 'right all along' about us, and hence it is very unlikely they will look at their own faults and make any changes for the better as a result of the incident. Regarding ourselves, the more 'awareness' we have, the more we will notice our negative responses and realise, 'whoops I've slid into that net again'. However, if we learn from the experience and endeavour to do better next time, it will have been worthwhile.

As discussed, due to the Law of like attracts like, we will keep attracting similar situations until we look at ourselves and make the necessary changes. It is important to stress again that it doesn't matter if the other person is right or wrong about us. Even being wrongly judged is an excellent Spiritual test for us (as discussed in the chapter on Humility), and is something that we have attracted. The 'victim' attitudes of poor, persecuted me, will directly keep us entwined in the web that we have become bound in. It will help tremendously if we can be mature enough to seek a higher perspective of the situation and ask ourselves, 'why have I attracted this and what weakness is it showing in me?' Should we humbly and sincerely do this we will get the answers. We will then actively desire to thank our adversary for exposing the aspect of ourselves on which we need to work. We can then, with real love, admit our faults and at the same time humbly apologise for 'not living our lives how they would have us live it' (which is normally the problem), and demonstrate sincere compassion and understanding for their feeling as they do towards us. We will never have to compromise our Truth or lives overall when we are humble and project back compassion and unconditional love in *all* circumstances.

It is for the reasons above that those closest to us often provide
the greatest challenge as to the lightening or darkening of our
Inner Density. Our emotions serve as crystal clear pointers as
to which way we are gravitating. Therefore, our family
generally gives us our greatest tests in 'letting go', (See
Footnote) and becoming detached from the transient to allow
the true love of God to work through us and touch *all* those
with whom we come into contact.

Take a son in a wealthy family who is good looking, and
naturally intelligent enough to coast through school. He has
no problem with women and due to his parent's contacts and
wealth, the way is paved before him for whatever job he wishes
to do - should he desire to work! He can easily afford a nice
house wherever he wishes to live and plenty of holidays. He
has the family security/cocoon to fall back on and bail him
out, and smooth the waters again for him should he get caught
for some minor outlandish crime, in whatever part of the globe.
Hence, provided he maintains the convention of the Family
and does not rock the boat too hard, he could get away with a
'lovely life' until he dies, and fair play to him. Such people
tend to be the envy of many a person, *but* what about in God's
eyes? And how does their Spirit feel?

It is very difficult for a person in such a position not to become
arrogant. Towards the end of Kafka's book, 'The Trial' (about
the very dense Lower Etheric, discussed in more detail in the
Chapter on Lucifer), when 'the Accused' knew his trial was
not going well, he was told by a lowly gentleman that everyone
in the courtroom knew he was doomed from Day One due to
'The shape of his mouth'. How many far reaching truths are
there in 'Old Wives Tales', such as - 'Don't keep putting on
that face or the wind'll change!' - 'The lofty looks of men
shall be humbled, and the haughtiness of men shall be bowed

down, and the Lord alone shall be exalted in that day.' Isaiah 2 vs 11.

However, with the Spirit Spark within us demanding action, movement and progress, imagine how such a person feels deep down, particularly as they move into their 30s and 40s, having never held down a proper job, or felt really needed and useful; with that niggly feeling in the back of the mind of, 'what's the point in earning a 'pittance' when I can dip into the family millions whenever I choose - a bit of sucking up is easier than the 9 to 5 grind'. He may feel frustrated and surplus to requirements to the murmurings of 'He's got a rich daddy', when his contemporaries from school are working hard to make ends meet off their own backs. 'The more a man strives for pleasure, the less pleasure he achieves.' 'For he that soweth to his flesh shall of the flesh reap corruption; but he that soweth to the Spirit shall of the Spirit reap life everlasting. And let us not be weary in well doing: for in due season we shall reap, if we faint not.' Galatians 6 vs 8 - 9.

Any stifling of the Spirit gives rise to a predominance of base emotions, attitudes and desires. Hence, there is no need to envy anyone - God is Omnipresent and all seeing:- 'For there is nothing covered that shall not be revealed; neither hid, that shall not be known.' Luke 12 vs 2. In God's eyes is such a person to be envied or pitied? And are the parents, in constantly smoothing the waters for their children, performing an act of love when love is the giving of yourself, not of possessions? This same principle applies, of course, to both rich and poor.

As we become more stifled and lazy, we become more selfish. When we are not pushing ourselves and putting our backs into whatever we are doing, our sharpness and awareness of our surroundings and others subtly (see 'Lucifer' Chapter) diminishes. The more insensitive and unobservant we become, the more we expect others to clean and wash up after us and generally put themselves out for us. This Lack of giving results in a dullness filtering into our being to the extent that we don't even notice if another is happy or sad inside, feels left out and needs a drink or some attention and so on. A clue lies in the word 'observant'; should we take the 'ob' away this leaves 'servant' which implies that the outcome of being observant is being sensitive, helpful and in service to others - and therefore God. 'Love thy neighbour as thyself.'

To be unobservant is to be selfish and indolent, with all the corresponding effects on our Spirit. Arrogance/snobbery is another consequence of being unobservant, whereby we tend to put people or groups of people into a 'bracket' and are scathing and undermining about them when speaking of them to others. Such an attitude means that we are 'judging' them with the subsequent damage to ourselves (see Chapter on Judgement), and when we focus mainly on the negative aspects of others, as opposed to the 'light behind the mask', this is a direct reflection of something within ourselves, which we then need to deal with if we are to 'Grow'.

Until we can let go (See *Footnote*) of our petty, egotistical hang ups and attitudes, can 'love' be anything other than possessive and/or obsessive, because of our awful sense of ownership, and all the corresponding hurtful breakdowns in human relationships induced by this? The natural shape of an elastic band is round, and how often do we try to pull it and stretch it, yet it always reverts to its original state, unless it snaps!

FOOTNOTE- Letting go: In order to master our future, we must first be master of our past. Letting go means coming to terms with, for example, guilt and then being at peace with it through understanding, forgiveness and so forth.

12. MAMMON

Mammon comprises all earthly and temporal things. It also comprises all idolatries. For example, the influence of the old 'Gods' and effigies have atrophied, and most are now just 'history'. These days western man, in particular, tends to idolise science, technology and money. However, if we can't keep such things in perspective, and believe we can walk (and sometimes bulldoze) through life putting our Faith in the above, then a situation will come into our lives where we will find that we are not able to cope without God's help.

'No man can serve two masters: for either he will hate the one and love the other; or else he will hold to the one and despise the other. Ye cannot serve God and Mammon.' Matthew 6 vs 24. Do we serve Our Will, or choose to align with God's? This is not to say material things cannot be used in accordance with God's Will, but it is very, very difficult:- 'That a rich man shall *hardly* enter into the Kingdom of Heaven. And again I say unto you, It is easier for a camel to go through the eye of a needle, than for a rich man to enter into the Kingdom of God.' Matthew 19 vs 23, 24. The temptations from any earthly pleasures, materially related or otherwise, to satisfy the base emotions and thereby stagnate in an artificial, cosy kind of security are very great.

When walking down a street and a drunken tramp approaches us and asks us for money, there are two questions we can ask ourselves should we decide to help. First, are we truly helping him by giving him money and even making him promise not to buy more alcohol? Or secondly, do we ask him what he wants, and if he says some tea and a bun, then go and buy him precisely that? As in all things, we must be prepared to take full responsibility for all our actions, including what and how we give to others.

Therefore, what of Christ's advice to the rich man to give all his worldly goods to the poor for the sake of his salvation? This concept could be interpreted in terms of if a person has wealth and a large home, they should at least open up their doors to as many tramps and people as want to enter in. The effects of such an action will mean that many tramps and all sorts of other people become dependent upon somebody else for their needs. 'Dependency' upon another, in certain situations (See *Footnote*), blocks our Spiritual Growth (as discussed in Chapter on The Family), and is avoiding taking responsibility for ourselves. (One exception is where an individual is dependent upon another as a result of severe physical or mental health problems - discussed in the final Chapter). The Spiritually content tramps are the ones who do not depend upon anybody else, even though in many ways they are suffering some of the biggest hardships in daily life.

'Render therefore unto Caesar the things which are Caesar's; and unto God the things which are God's.' Matthew 22 vs 21. Personal Responsibility means we will reap the corresponding Karma if we don't pay our debts and taxes, whether we feel this is right or wrong. 'Every man also to whom God hath given riches and wealth, and hath given him power to eat thereof, and to take his portion, and to rejoice in his labour; this is the gift of God.' Ecclesiastes 5 vs 19. Wealth is, of course, a *gift*, and those who are wealthy have a responsibility to use it in accordance with God's Will for the benefit of others and the planet, and *not* for purely *selfish needs*. Furthermore, the more we have the greater our responsibility:- 'For unto whomsoever much is given, of him shall be much required: and to whom men have committed much, of him they will ask more.' Luke 12 vs 48.

In the light of the above, it could be construed that if a 'rich man' gave all his money away, then this is a 'cop out' of his responsibility/gift. Taking the current, very popular lottery as an example. Does winning twenty million pounds do an average person any favours? There are many lottery winners who undergo a drastic change of lifestyle, but then may struggle to hold on to their 'purpose in life'. This is made even harder by the many temptations presented to them by their own 'dreams and fantasies' and the sudden influx of new 'friends' eager to get to know them. Therefore, some fairly heavy Karma is more often than not the result, unless handled in accordance with God's Will. It must also be remembered that such an apparent windfall is, as in all things, not a coincidence and provides a great challenge for the Spiritual development of the 'lucky' winner!

The overriding point concerning Mammon is whether we use our 'gift' how God would have us use it, or whether we become possessive, greedy, selfish, lazy and/or arrogant:- 'For where your treasure is, there will be your heart also.' Matthew 6 vs 21. When Christ told the rich man to give all his worldly goods away and follow him, this was because it was the best thing this individual could do for his salvation. The 'rich man' represents those people who follow and keep well all the Laws and meet all requirements, pay their dues, do good to others and are comfortably off or rich themselves. This is a lot of people. They are not bad, in fact most can be considered kind, helpful, considerate, friendly, charitable and so forth. *But*, if their own wealth or comfort, secure livelihood, house and

154

savings were threatened, they can suddenly change. They are willing to give, but not everything, as was the case with Ananias and Sapphira in Acts 5. They are willing to help others, but not at the cost of their own lives. They are willing to suffer, but only if they have something to fall back on.

'No man can serve two masters ...' No doubt had Christ asked the rich man to give ten, twenty, even fifty per cent of his worldly goods away, then this man would have eagerly obliged. If we are one who is entrenched in the luxuries of mammon and attached to the apparent benefits, such as feeling our personality and social status to be dependent upon our material wealth - relishing the admiration and even envy of acquaintances, and being able to buy most or all the fruits of our desires, then it won't hurt to seriously ask what Christ might say to us should we ask him, 'What good thing shall I do, that I may have eternal life?'

'And Jesus sat over against the treasury, and beheld how the people cast money into the treasury: and many that were rich cast in much. And there came a certain poor widow, and she threw in two mites, which make a farthing. And he called unto him his disciples, and saith unto them, Verily I say unto you, That this poor widow hath cast more in than all they which have cast into the treasury: For all they did cast in of their abundance; but she of her want did cast in all that she had, even all her living.' Mark 12 vs 41 - 44. Giving, as in all things, is Karmically related. This means whether we give with Love and Faith in God and hence love for our neighbour, as is the case with the poor lady who truly gave of herself, or give with an inner feeling of, 'getting God off our backs until we have time to really start looking for Him and His Will in our lives'.

Any charity is, of course, very much better than no charity and the world currently needs as much charity as we all of us are willing to give. However, it is important to realise that God knows exactly what we all have in our 'bank accounts', and the extent to which we truly and sincerely give of ourselves with love and compassion. Karma is also related to how ostentatious we are in our giving - to be seen by others as a generous, kind individual. 'He that speaketh of himself seeketh his own glory: but he that seeketh his glory that sent him, the same is true, and no unrighteousness is in him.' John 7 vs 18.

As mentioned any possessiveness or envy/jealousy of another is allowing Lucifer into our hearts, which has the corresponding affect on our Inner Density:- 'Thou shalt not covet thy neighbour's house, nor anything that is thy neighbour's.' Exodus 20 vs 17. Complete respect for everyone and everything is the way forward. *But*, a warning in the words of Solomon, 'Through envy of the Devil came Death into the world.'

If all our worldly goods are suddenly stripped away, know that this too is Divine Intention Karmically speaking, and an example of God's love and mercy. It may be to shatter our ego, which has become dependent on a flash car or ostentatious objects of material status, or to shake our Spirit, which has stagnated in a cosy cocoon without us necessarily realising it, in order to get us moving and growing again:- 'The life of man upon the earth is a trial.' Job. In Pilgrim's Progress, the Valley of Ease is very short if the person is on the path of a 'True' Christian, before being given the next set of lessons. How often does it happen, that once we feel happy and maybe even a little smug at overcoming something, than the next day - *wham*! our next trial hits us?

'But seek ye first the Kingdom of God and his righteousness; and all these things shall be added unto you.' Matthew 6 vs

33. When we are genuinely aligned with God's Will, our Mammon and earthly needs will be provided for us - the same as they are for the 'Sparrows and all the fowls of the air' etc. 'He that trusteth in his riches shall fall: but the righteous shall flourish as a branch.' Proverbs 11 vs 28.

The above message concerning Mammon is constantly repeated throughout the Bible, and is mostly clearly summarised in 1 Timothy 6 vs 8 - 10:- 'And having food and raiment let us be therewith content. But they that will be rich fall into temptation and a snare, and into many foolish and hurtful lusts, which drown men in destruction and perdition. For the *love* of money is the root of all evil: which while some coveted after, they have erred from the faith, and pierced themselves through with many sorrows.' 'Loving' money means hoarding it, which makes us greedy, selfish and sometimes deceitful, and flaunting it via extravagant luxuries, and enjoying the self-esteem via the adoration/admiration and envy of others.

The more our personality, character and self-worth becomes dependent upon or attached to our material status, making us haughty, arrogant, smug and so on, the greater our bondage to Lucifer becomes. 'Charge them that are rich in this world, that they be not highminded, nor trust in uncertain riches, but in the living God, who giveth us richly all things to enjoy: That they do good, that they be rich in good works, ready to distribute, willing to communicate; Laying up in store for themselves a good foundation against the time to come, that they may lay hold on eternal life.' 1 Timothy 6 vs 17 - 19.

FOOTNOTE: The word 'Dependency' in this book means an unhealthy dependence upon another or situation, whereby if things don't work out how we would like or expect them to, we feel completely lost for a while. The more we then feel such emotions as self-pity, anger, bitterness and blame, the more damage we inflict upon ourselves. However, we all depend upon each other for different things in our daily lives. For example, regarding our job we are dependent upon our boss for our wages in the same way as he depends on us to do our job as well as we can to help maintain the objectives of the business. The point is that the only one we can totally depend upon is God:- 'It is better to trust in the Lord than to put confidence in man.' Psalm 118 vs 8. The chapter on Work stresses the need for flexibility of mind and an openness of heart if we are to avoid damage resulting from unforeseen future circumstances, due to an unhealthy dependence on our part.

13. TOOLS AND GIFTS

The Bible speaks of, 'All Divination being Abomination', in the Old Testament. However, in the New Testament, 1 Corinthians 12 vs 9-10 states ' .... to another the gifts of healing by the same Spirit; To another the working of miracles: to another prophecy: to another discerning of Spirits ....' Could this be yet another Biblical contradiction? And does Discerning of Spirits mean discerning so they can be used properly in accordance with God's Will? And what is the difference between Divination and Prophecy - if any? (The 'Discerning of Spirits' is the gift of discerning whether something is of God or of Lucifer or of a person's own making).

First, it should be noted that many religions (including some of the major ones) outside of Christianity quite happily and openly use a variety of divinatory techniques. However, the Bible is correct about what it says about Divination, in so much as were it possible for a Tarot reader to tell someone their precise future, it could deprive their Spirit of the full Karmic effect necessary for their growth, and consequently both parties would receive Reciprocal Action. However, there can be beneficial aspects of divining. For example, when doing a tarot reading and we get 'Death', which means drastic changes, representing our 'broad' future, we can be more mentally prepared for something transformative within us, our surroundings and frequently both. Likewise, the 8 of discs in our 'recommended future', would be advising us to take things step by step - no radical leaps or moves.

Divination is 'Abomination' in the sense that Diviners use tools or systems which they have to devise and create; i.e. the diviner's means of Divination is man-made, and thus it has all the limitations that this fact imposes. Divination by Astrology, for example, is determined only by the stars and/or planets that man can see from or are relatively close to the earth, but there are countless more stars out there which we can't see and some may exert more influence than our whole Solar System put together. The Tarot is both a tool and a system. It has been handed down through the ages, during which distortions are bound to have occurred - remember the telephone game, when a sentence is whispered to a person on their left or right and passed around a room full of people, how it distorts and changes en route.

It was mentioned in the Definitions chapter that the principal purpose of the Tarot could well have been to preserve the hidden Truths in pictorial forms. This was so as to give it a greater chance of surviving the passage of time with minimal distortions. Psalm 119 contains 22 'sections' - the same as the number of major Arcana in a pack of Tarot cards. Most of the sections bear a strong similarity to the modern day meanings of the respective Tarot Cards. For example, the Fool is the first card of the majors and verse 1, Psalm 119 (Aleph) reads, 'Blessed are the undefiled in the way, who walk in the law of the Lord.' This equals The Fool. The Fool is a seeker, innocent in mind, who 'listens' to the song of his heart then follows it without hesitation, and is more open to the promptings of the Spirit and God.

Similarly Psalms 1 to 22 bear many similarities to the 22 major Arcana. Assuming Psalm 1 corresponds to the Fool (even though the Fool in a Tarot deck is number zero, there is no corresponding Psalm zero), Psalm 1 verses 1 - 3 reads:-

'Blessed is the man that walketh not in the counsel of the ungodly, nor standeth in the way of sinners, nor sitteth in the seat of the scornful. But his delight is in the law of the Lord; and in his law doth he meditate day and night. And he shall be like a tree planted by the rivers of water, that bringeth forth his fruit in his season; his leaf also shall not wither; and whatsoever he doeth shall prosper.' Psalm 22 would correspond to The World, the last of the major Arcana cards, which means; fulfilment, the culmination of a cycle after a severe and testing journey giving rise to renewal and timeless joy throughout the hearts of all orders of creation. Psalm 22 contains the prophesies regarding the completion of Christ's life on earth and his crucifixion, beginning at verse 1, which reads:- 'My God, my God, why hast thou forsaken me?' and verses 16 and 18 respectively:- 'For dogs have compassed me: the assembly of the wicked have inclosed me: they pierced my hands and my feet. They part my garments among them, and cast lots upon my vesture.'

The Tarot is believed to have originated in Egypt, where Moses spent considerable time studying and learning over 3,500 years ago, and it contains many wonderful and hidden Truths, cleverly preserved in pictorial form, which has helped it to survive the passage of time. It is likely that the most important function of the Tarot is as a book of 'Ancient Knowledge'. Moreover, in Egyptian, Ta-rot is said to mean 'Royal Road', which is the Spiritual Path in the most direct sense.

For people to say that all Tarot cards, and other Divinatory systems, are solely 'Tools of the Devil', is a narrow-minded and fear-orientated Judgement, and reveals a lack of Faith in God's Omnipresence in every being and thing. However, Tarot can indeed be a tool of the Devil - it's a pack of cards and as such it is materialistic. So like any materialistic 'gift' - money, television or car, it can be used for good or ill. A car can be used to run someone over or as an ambulance to take somebody to hospital; our choice, responsibility and Reciprocal Action. Being materialistic, the Tarot is more easily manipulated by the Devil than by God, because it is man, by his own will who has to interpret the cards, and this is the point where the 'Devil' has a better chance of throwing a 'spanner in the works'.

The main way in which Tarot can be an abomination is when it distracts people from looking to God and they begin to rely on it in no matter how small a way. Even if the cards are correct, they may sometimes refer to a different situation to what we may think, and if someone depends upon or acts upon the outcome of the cards, they may well slip up on a banana skin. However, provided we are seeking to align with God's Will, we'll learn a valuable lesson.

On the whole it is easy to say such 'Tools' should, if used at all, be taken very lightly and solely as a point of interesting comparison. *But*, who are we to say any shoulds and shouldn'ts? For example, many people get invaluable help from a good Taroist as they would from a good psychiatrist. There are many cases of Taroists averting the course of someone who is potentially suicidal and getting them to view life with a different positive attitude. The Taroist has the benefit of 'seeing' the suicide mentality in the cards before the person has spoken, and can focus the counselling accordingly.

Likewise, Mediums can play the part of an invaluable catalyst in another's Spiritual Growth, by simply proving to them that there is life after death which gets them on the path of seeking for themselves. Further encouragement may be gained from a useful message and the fact that it is certainly not boring on the other side - the relation or friend often can't stay too long because they're very busy working. Also, many of them bear none of their old grudges and hang-ups, depending on their level of Inner Density. For example, those entrenched in the Lower Etheric will still be holding on to and projecting all the base emotions that were dominant whilst they were on earth. However, those in the Mid and High Ethereal Realms will be more focused on working towards the light, in which case they will have grown and developed following their 'judgement' at physical death.

The purpose of many funeral services throughout various religions, such as Christian, Tibetan and Ancient Egyptian, is centred along the very beneficial lines of freeing the Spirit of the person from their body and the earth (should they still be clinging on), and encouraging their loved ones also to let go and allow the 'dead' to go on their new journey. So is mediumship work binding Spirits (wrapped in their 'Ethereal Cloaks') to earth and preventing them from passing on to their next stage?

In our immense grief, we can consciously or otherwise 'hold on' to our loved ones and prevent them from 'moving on'. Such people will sometimes mention they feel their 'presence' round them all the time and may even claim to 'talk to them'. It is in this situation when it must be asked whether we are doing our loved ones any favours! Likewise, when a Medium tries to contact a specific person for someone, such as their Uncle Tim, could the medium not be potentially interrupting something important that he's doing at the time to satisfy our own selfish needs and insecurities, and thereby indirectly act as a disturbance and hindrance for him?

However, when the Medium doesn't try to contact any specific person, it's the Spirit's choice whether it makes contact or not - nobody's forcing it, and therefore can it be said that the Medium is damaging the Spirit in any way? This is particularly true since a Spirit never stays in 'open contact' for longer than it has to, *unless* the entity is after something itself, and the Medium is not in control. Therefore, in this situation, is not the only potential danger to us, not the Entity?

With regard to 'Channelling', there are many people today who can go into a trance-like state and allow another to speak through them, *but* there are endless warnings, particularly from Jesus himself:- 'For many shall come in my name, saying, I am Christ; and shall deceive many. And many false prophets shall rise, and shall deceive many,' Matthew 24 vs 5 and 11.

The law of Inner Density means it is impossible to contact beings lighter or higher than yourself. Hence, beware of 'Channellers' who are clearly confused, and who claim to channel 'very high beings'; there are people who claim to channel so called supposed Ascended Masters, Archangels, Jesus and even God. There are many con-merchants in both our world and the next, who can easily deceive the ego of such a Channeller, when they open themselves to what they believe to be a Divine entity.

However, who are we to say they're not channelling an Archangel? What we can be sure of is that they will not be channelling such a being direct, because, according to Inner Density, if a message were to come down, it would have to come through a series of 'mediators', - the last one being through a Spirit at a *similar level of denseness* as the one channelling. Hence, if the channel's heart is contaminated, deceitful and dishonest, his/her Spirit would be aligned to the Lower Etheric, and who knows what distortions in the message this 'final mediator' may make.

According to the law of equilibrium, a more powerful being,

entity or Spirit can come through a person who is somewhat weaker, whether that person believes in such things or not. This law would also allow a more powerful being of the light to do the same thing, but morally they would not unless it were of the utmost importance to God's overall intention and designs.

The major difference between the above and those who 'channel' is that heavenly beings contact us. We cannot contact them as and when we feel like it. Also, it doesn't matter if we're meditating or doing the shopping, due to the power of the light and the importance of the message/act. For example, the conversion of Saul occurred as he was walking down the road to Damascus, when he was bathed in a 'light from Heaven', Acts 9. Similar examples are the Archangel Gabriel appearing to Mary to tell her to take Jesus away to escape King Herod, and the angel freeing the chains of Peter in Acts 12.

Prophets such as Isaiah, Daniel, Jeremiah and even the occasional modern day individual such as Nostradamus, who have made correct prophecy's on a global scale (aeroplanes being Nostradamus' most obvious prophecy) have 'been given' a sample of the world's Destiny - big D, for the benefit of mankind. The early prophets, in particular, predicted events accurately hundreds, and even thousands of years into the future. This is because God allowed them a glimpse of the Global Wheel. The Universe is perfectly structured and *logical*, but the way 'time' works in the Universe is different to our understanding of it and therefore very difficult for us to comprehend.

When man opted for the Karmic Path instead of the Path of Love, then the overall Destiny for mankind naturally took root - as discussed earlier. This means that no individual or country can change or alter the future - globally speaking, in any way. We only have to look at how many people have tried to influence the 'Global Wheel' over the course of history - and failed. Napolean Bonaparte, a man who'd spent his life trying to change the course of history, recognised this just before he died, when he said, "Do you know what astonished me most in the world? The inability of force to create anything. In the long run the sword is always beaten by the Spirit."

There is a monumental difference between the ever moving Global Wheel and our own individual Karmic wheels, which move up and down depending on the way we cope with the circumstances presented to us. We can fight against the 'Global Wheel', try to manipulate, change or even control it - this is our *Free Will*. However, as mentioned, we won't succeed and we will build up more Karma in the process - it's a bit of a cheek to think we know better than God as to the direction the world should go. Therefore, our role within the Global Wheel can be likened to being in a play, whereby depending upon our performance and what we put into it, in alignment with how we're directed, we are either booed or applauded at the end.

Clairvoyants, tarot readers and such like 'tune into' an individual's wheel which is rotating within the overall wheel. They can sometimes 'see' a person's circumstances weeks, months, and even years into the future. The circumstances 'created' for each individual are directly related to how they've dealt with their life/lives up until then - Karma, destiny little 'd' (as discussed). Because we have Free Will, we can change the impact of future circumstances and even the event itself by the way we conduct ourselves between now and then. Future events are therefore based on our current attitudes and Spiritual needs, and if, for example, we have a surge of inspiration resulting in a radical change in our attitude, then a certain 'planned' future event may no longer be necessary or it may alter. It is for this reason that a clairvoyant/tarot reader's accuracy decreases the further they predict into the future.

An example of this in operation is when a Tarot reader tells a client that in six months they will have considerable monetary wealth, and the person then sits back, relaxes and is broke in six months time. The Tarot readers' reading was based on the individual continuing down their current path with their current attitude. It would appear that such a person would have been better off without the reading, but if they learn that they can't rely and depend upon anything or anybody other than God, then the experience may be a good thing - Karmically speaking!

By far and a way our most valuable asset is our *intuitive perception*, which we can work on developing through meditation and/or stilling ourselves for a period every day, and emptying our minds of our mundane daily thoughts. We can then allow the light of God to fill our bodies through our heart or the top of our head which, in combination with our conscience, enables us to '*feel*' or inwardly know what is right and wrong for us. Hence, *leave the judgement of others actions to God and His Will.* This is what we would do if we had real *faith*, because we would know that everybody receives the daily lessons appropriate for them, with the corresponding Reciprocal Action, which will give them the 'opportunity' to grow. 'For what man knoweth the things of a man, but the Spirit of a man which is in him? even so the things of God knoweth no man, but the Spirit of God. Now we have received, not the Spirit of the world, but the Spirit which is of God; that we might know the things that are freely given to us of God.' 1 Corinthians 2 vs 11, 12.

HOW DO WE KNOW WHO'S GENUINE AND WHO'S NOT?

The answer is in the points above:- 'Wherefore by their *fruits* ye shall know them,' Matthew 7 vs 20, and, 'Beware of false Prophets, which come to you in sheep's clothing, but inwardly they are ravening wolves.' Matthew 7 vs 15 - i.e. if the channeller, medium or whoever is really nice to you *but* wants *anything* from you, whether it be money (over and above a small donation towards living expenses), a place to stay, or even that you should believe in them in no matter how small a way - *question their integrity*.

The *ego* is the biggest clue to showing up a False Prophet, and if you listen carefully, the 'channelling' can sometimes contain material they have read, knowingly or unknowingly, in books, the message may stutter in places instead of simply flowing and there may be a lot of talk on the 'bliss out' lines of multi-dimensional, multi-facetted realities from our Solar System to the furthest stars. This may well distract those involved from the all important here and now, and from taking full responsibility for themselves and it may provide another form of escape (like drugs). If such gifts, in fuelling the ego, make us or the channeller strut around like peacocks in a chicken run, and we are taken in due to our Indolence, *all* will reap the corresponding Reciprocal Action.

Another common facet is the 'Crisis mentality' - getting excited about global disasters, whether it be a third World War, or the St Andreas Fault about to crack sending California into the Pacific, with an underlying attitude of, 'See I told you so, now you will bow down and listen to my message'.

If we are taken in by a False Prophet, then as in all things we have attracted this situation into our lives. However, provided our volition is pure and for the good we will learn an invaluable lesson in the 'Discernment of Spirit' and people, when we see through and overcome the challenge.

An example of a good modern day channeller/medium is Mary Margaret-Moore, who channels an energy she calls 'Bartholomew'. Mary Margaret-Moore approaches channelling from a down to earth, practical angle, and constantly stresses the 'living in the here and now and being alive and aware in the moment'. This is confirmed by Jesus:- 'Take therefore no thought for the morrow: for the morrow shall take thought for the things of itself. Sufficient unto the day is the evil thereof,' Matthew 6 vs 34, and the late Bob Marley: 'If you know what life is worth you will look for yours on earth and now you see the light, you must stand up for your rights.' However, he also warned: 'Many people will fight you down when you see the light,' as did Jesus:- 'And ye shall be hated of all men for my name's sake: but he that endureth to the end shall be saved.' Matthew 10 vs 22. It is very easy to 'bliss out' in Spirit; the hard part is to bring it back down into our beings and anchor our Spirit here on earth to live according to the Will of God.

14. LUCIFER

Lucifer is not some big bad monster who when he 'touches' someone, makes their eyes glow red, as portrayed in some movies. If it were black and white like this, then we'd have little problem in coping with evil, if we wanted to. The Lucifer energy is very subtle and slippery, and tickles our pampered ego and the feelings of, 'once I have enough money and am in control, then I'll turn myself to God's ways of loving my neighbour and the planet'. Such *lukewarmness*, even though we might be 'nice people with good intentions', is not going to help our Spirit to progress.

As we make more money, it is easy to become more entrenched in Mammon, such as the little luxuries that become part of our daily lives, so that it becomes harder and harder to break free from our habits and *make the time* to find God in our lives. When we hear ourselves saying, 'once I've paid for such and such then I will start embodying God's Will in my life', or, 'I'll start once I've made just enough for one more good holiday', we'll know that we're not on the track of Truth.

Such compromising of the Truth is one of the most effective means by which the Lucifer energy filters into our beings and stalls our Spiritual Growth. The more this happens, the more we hold on to the things of the earth such as other people and our material security, and the result is our Faith diminishes relative to this. Even though we may be successful in our earthly pursuits, when we are in such situations we will become less happy inside as the light around our Spirit becomes duller and duller - this hurts! It is then that we begin to seek more earnestly for praise from others concerning our deeds and the way we conduct ourselves, whether we be funny, clever or so on, and we allow the light of God to be gradually squeezed from our beings. 'But God knoweth your hearts, for that which is highly esteemed among men, is Abomination in the sight of God.' Luke 16 vs 15. As this happens we will get a niggly feeling of guilt and frustration deep within us because we're not truly living our lives how God would have us live.

It is in such situations that we look to make 'compromises' with God to 'buy some more time' before we sincerely start to align, look within and change some fairly major aspects of our character we already 'know' don't meet with His approval! For example, we may write a 'generous' cheque out for some charity, and then are unable to resist telling others (even though we know this is not quite right). However, 'for the time being it really is more important that our friends and acquaintances see our charity, so at least they think more highly of us'. To take the example of the poor widow discussed in the Chapter on Mammon:- 'Verily I say unto you, That this poor widow hath cast more in, than all they which have cast into the treasury: For all they did cast in of their abundance; but she of her want did cast in all that she had, even all her living.' Mark 12 vs 43, 44.

It will help to keep asking ourselves questions such as, 'am I doing what I'm doing for my own ego - to be thought more highly of by others?' And, 'am I doing this or that to try to fulfil others' expectations of me?' Should our parents be the type who will only be truly proud of us when we are a carbon copy of them, it doesn't matter how hard we try, we will never wholly succeed. For example, should we become the Managing Director of a big company, then, in their eyes, we may not be conducting our private life 'correctly', such as not spending enough time with our family. Hence, the most important question we can ask ourselves in such situations is, 'are we doing what we are doing for God and to align with His Will, or to satisfy and gain approval from our parents and/or other people?'

Some feel that the higher we rise to the light, the more we 'attract' the power of Lucifer into our lives - equal and opposite. This in effect is true, because our Spirit in alignment with God's Will attracts whatever tests we need corresponding to our level of Inner Density, and hence our tests are those which we can just cope with if we tackle them correctly - the lighter we are the greater the tests *appear* to be. For example, there would be little benefit to the progress of a Spiritually advanced person if they lost their passport or wallet. In this situation, the potential Karmic benefit would more than likely be for the individual who finds it, and how they cope with the obvious temptations.

Such tests will continue until we attain a state of unconditional love and selflessness; i.e. all forgiving and commending all our 'worthy' deeds to God, and not even taking the merest speck of credit ourselves. How often when we have done something creditable, and endeavour to point to God, do we take ten per cent for ourselves and a pat on the back. *But*, if we open our eyes in God awareness, we may notice two little horns growing on our heads, or on the head of the one who's patting us.

There is only the *one energy*, which can be directed or used for different purposes. Likewise, we can use the energy created by God for good or evil. It is for these reasons that 'evil' can be defined as simply 'undeveloped good'.

174

'For he maketh his sun to rise on the evil and on the good, and sendeth rain on the just and on the unjust.' Matthew 5 vs 45. This suggests that 'Lucifer' works for God. 'I form the light and create darkness: I make peace and create evil: I the Lord do all these things.' Isaiah 45 vs 7. God knew the possibilities when He gave man Free Will and in His love for us made the Garden of Eden the ultimate in beauty. All Adam and Eve had to do was resist eating of the 'Tree of Knowledge of Good and Evil', as discussed earlier. Hence, God did everything He could to make the 'path of love' as appealing as possible, and overwhelmingly hoped man wouldn't abuse his Freedom. This was demonstrated by His immediate reaction of disappointment and despair when Adam and Eve succumbed to temptation, Genesis 3 vs 8 - 19.

Translated literally, Lucifer means 'Light Bearer', and it is his nature to *tempt* in whatever way he can, and he's *brilliant* at it. Our Spirit in accordance with the Four Laws will attract the necessary situations into our lives to show us our weak points which we need to work on. Lucifer most often exerts his influence when we're at our weakest, such as when we're very tired and ill, or when we think we are on top, or when we are covetous. But, all he can do is tempt. Christ put himself to the ultimate test by going out into the wilderness for forty days and nights without food and confronted Lucifer direct: - When we're both tired and very hungry, temptations increase exponentially.

'But if thine eye be evil, thy whole body shall be full of darkness. If therefore the light that is in thee be darkness, how great is the darkness.' Matthew 6 vs 23. Some of the most dangerous people, in whom the Lucifer Energy is most deeply entrenched, are those who are convinced they are working for God, but 'if the light that is in thee be darkness, how great is that darkness'. Such seeds are sown in some Spiritual Groups who contact those in the next life and then feel they are 'just a little more Spiritual' than their neighbour. Likewise, when religious groups are convinced their methods of worship are superior, in however small a way, to those of another. It's our Spirit and Inner Density which suffers if we choose evil before good, and it combines with similar energies (Law of Attraction). Therefore, in a global sense Lucifer has his claws well and truly embedded; re. Mammon, man's greed and Base Emotions. 'For ye are yet carnal: for whereas there is among you envying, and strife, and divisions, are ye not carnal, and walk as men?' 1 Corinthians 3 vs 3.

This directly affects the level to which we 'gravitate' after Physical death, as mentioned in the Definitions earlier. An example of one level of 'Hell', is the one to which souls gravitate who have led a lustful/conceited/arrogant life or were thieves or other types of 'bad' people. This level is brilliantly invoked by Kafka's book and film 'The Trial', where everybody is sordid, confused, and fearful. It portrays thousands of people sitting in silence and contemplating, whilst they wait indefinitely for just the first hearing of their trial. (See *Footnote*). Being 'trapped' in limbo combined with their denseness, means these 'souls' suffer what feels like every second of our time the way we perceive it, whereas Spirits higher up exist in a different perception, and therefore experience, of space and time. We all of us get a glimpse of this in our daily lives. For example, when we're doing something laborious time seems to drag, but when we are doing something enjoyable the time seems to fly by.

In such a situation, it is not difficult to comprehend why given the opportunity, such Spirits reincarnate into a life of starvation in Ethiopia or torture in Communist China, in the knowledge that through their suffering they can cast off a huge amount of their Karmic burden (built up through their misdemeanours in previous lives) and rise, in a very short space and time, to a level far higher than where they were. It may also be that the individual needs this last short, sharp shock, to release their last pieces of Karma so that they can leave the Karmic Cycle for good and return 'home' as a mature Spirit. This is another example of God's wonderful forgiveness and love for mankind.

The moving of objects by poltergeists is little more than a cry for help *to us*. It is possible for us to help these Spirits by listening to them and hearing what they have to say - for example, by bringing in experienced priests or mediums who deal with this sort of phenomena. Should the entity humbly confess their sins and/or trauma, and thereby forgive themselves and/or others, their Spirit may be freed to move on to pastures new, and they will no longer need to switch the pictures on the wall, or whatever pranks it may tend to do. This can be potentially very *dangerous* for us if we ourselves try to deal with this sort of thing without experience. We can never be certain of the nature of what we're dealing with, and if we have a 'weakness', we can leave ourselves open to the potentially evil qualities of such Spirits and become partially possessed. The 'weakness' can often be seen as holes in our auras. Auras are our natural defence against Lower Etheric nasties, but if we take drugs, and/or excessive alcohol, we can 'blow holes' in our aura as we become more run down. The same principle applies to people who are very subdued and introverted, as a result of some kind of trauma. In extreme cases such people may not be able to make decisions for themselves and their auric strength may weaken relatively, and they will thus be more open to Etheric beings, particularly if they dabble with such things.

Could this be one of the causes of schizophrenia, in addition to the scientifically proven concept of chemical imbalance in the brain? 'Behold, I cast out devils, and I do cures today and tomorrow.' Luke 13 vs 32 - Jesus was forever casting out evil Spirits as much as he was curing physical ailments. Such entities latch on to an open and/or weak person to draw on their *energies* (which gives them a boost and delays the moment they look within, which one day they will have to do). This is similar to a tapeworm, which having wedged itself in someone's small intestine, sucks the life blood for its own growth oblivious of the harm it's doing to its host.

The early symptoms of such a 'parasite' are a strange sort of high, which may put us off our food and drink and result in slightly abnormal thoughts and behaviour. However, if it is not dealt with, it will take more of a hold, like any drug or parasite. For example, should we hear voices in our head, they may get louder and more demanding with time, and/or if we develop an urge to do something that we know is intrinsically wrong, this urge may get less controllable unless checked.

Another example is the like attracts like principle regarding a heavy drinker. As a clear-headed person attracts other clear-headed people and etheric beings, so a fuzzy headed person attracts like people and entities. However, as the individual drinks more, needing a 'tot' for breakfast to keep them going until an early liquid lunch, they and their protective aura become weaker, and they spend yet more time with similar people, as the corresponding attraction to like minded beings becomes stronger. The weaker they become, the less controllable and more irritable they get - quicker to anger/aggression and sadness/guilt and so on. Old friends can only help in this situation if such people are prepared to help themselves. There is a fine line, which varies from one individual to the next, but generally speaking when the person can no longer control their body, thoughts and feelings, then they are totally open to Etheric Parasites and spend much more of their time talking to .... themselves? However, it is vital that we don't blame outside propensities for the 'condition' in ourselves or others. Personal Responsibility is still of paramount necessity and it helps to remember that nothing can destroy our Spirit except God:- 'Fear not them which kill the body, but are not able to kill the soul: but rather fear him which is able to destroy both soul and body in hell.' Matthew 10 vs 28.

EXORCISM:- Self-exorcism is possible in the above situations provided we confront 'our guest' direct (as is the case with any disease or problem), and exert our strength over it with a genuine volition for the Light of God. Darkness cannot survive in the Light, *but* according to the Law of Equilibrium, we must be strong enough to bring in more light than the darkness to overcome it. The concept of, 'where your attention goes your energy flows', is again applicable. For example, the more we listen to 'voices' in our heads the more dominant they will become. The way to overcome them is to cut off their *energy* supply, which comes directly from us. This will necessitate a genuine heartfelt desire to be rid of these propensities and the strength to persist, overpower them and take no notice of what they say, no matter how hard things may get. Any parasite will not like it if its source of energy or food is reduced and it will then try to embed itself all the more at first, then later it will weaken through lack of 'nourishment' and will die or leave.

Fortunately, on Earth there are those who can help us, whose hearts are full of love, purity and courage with a rock solid Faith in God, and in who's name they cast out these Spirits. But, as in all things, we sometimes have to fight for what we want, and this simply doesn't lie in letting another fight our battles for us - the more we contribute the better, as Jesus kept saying:- 'Thy faith hath saved thee,' Luke 18 vs 42.

To summarise, there appear to be two main forms of exorcism:-
(a) The 'Caring' approach - listening to what a person or a Spirit has to say and encouraging a confession, to help them free their Spirit. Likewise, with regard to exorcising personal 'demons' such as guilt, anger, lust, self-pity, self-indulgence and any 'foreign' matter, whereby confession, confiding and talking to someone trustworthy can help to free our Spirit. (b) The Law of Equilibrium - Focusing our strength and all our energy over an Entity, whether it be in ourselves, another, or somebody's house - and simply sending it away. This can be done by anything from shouting it out and almost 'laying into it', to a Holy Ritual, (discussed in the final section of this Chapter). The underlying principle of the stronger mass overcoming the weaker mass still applies, because exorcism will only work if we have made ourselves stronger than our adversary. This may seem daunting *but*, it will help tremendously to remember that *love* is the dominant, most powerful energy in the universe.

TEENAGERS can be particularly susceptible to such Entities. This is because their minds and Spirits are developing very rapidly at this age and consequently they can often be more open to any old Tom, Dick or Harry in the Lower Etheric than an adult. As mentioned, such Entities, being very dense, still possess many of the Base Emotions, such as anger, and the horror stories we hear tend to be a result of the frustration of the Spirit, which feels that it is being 'messed around' by excited humans *dabbling* in what they don't understand. There are also some 'nasty pieces of work' out there and given the choice, it would be best to leave well alone. If we do choose to tackle a problem to try to help another, as in all things we must take full responsibility, but if we should have one iota of doubt, avoid any attempts at all costs. The best armour we have is our *faith in God*.

BLACK MAGICIANS:- It was mentioned that Lucifer's nature is to tempt, and the more we practice Black Magic, with the intention of harming another or influencing their thoughts in some way - for destructive purposes, our own benefits, or any reason, the more Satan will just laugh at our folly.

Lucifer knows God is all powerful, and that His light rules and dominates the Universe and that furthermore, he is merely working for God's Creation in providing us with the tests we need for our growth:- 'And when he went forth to land, there met him out of a city a certain man, which had devils long time, and wore no clothes, neither abode in any house, but in the tombs. When he saw Jesus he cried out, and fell down before him, and with a loud voice said, 'What have I to do with thee, Jesus, thou Son of God most high? I beseech thee, torment me not." Luke 8 vs 27 - 28. Evil bows down in front of True Light.

The more people give themselves up to Lucifer, which is unquestionably the easiest thing to do, the less he respects them. So those who look for reward from their 'Dear Lord Lucifer' will certainly receive it in the only form in which he can give it. As God rewards goodness with good things - joy, light and happiness, Satan rewards Satanists with yet more evil, darkness, eternal damnation, suffering and misery.

RITES AND RITUALS are more powerful than we most of us realise. We cannot have too much respect or exert too much caution when embarking on any form of ritual. The light of God is without question the dominant force in the Universe as mentioned, hence the Christian communion is an effective, powerful ritual for linking and opening up to God's universal love and bringing this love into our hearts and surroundings.

There are, of course, similar rites and rituals in most religions, which work on the same principles.

However, whilst on earth with Free Will, we are potentially subject to the darker forces in the Lower Etheric and the Lucifer energy in general. These can destroy us if we allow them to take control of our beings (which is what makes earth incarnations such a perfect testing ground to prove our worth to God). This will happen, for example, when we totally succumb to Black Magic Rituals and any similar, allowing our Base nature to envelop and dominate our thoughts, words and deeds. Such rituals can often involve 'sacrifices' and various sexual carnal pursuits.

The Law of Attraction. There are certain Cults and Churches that are obsessed with Satan and invest tremendous amounts of energy attempting to expel evil from their surroundings and evil Spirits from their followers. Unfortunately, forces of a like energy actually feed and grow in these situations. This makes those involved put more energy into 'fighting evil', giving these forces yet more energy, and a vicious circle results.

We can all of us see this same principle at work in our day to day lives when dealing with our thoughts. Should we have a negative thought which is bothering us, the more we try to fight it and strive not to think about it, the more this thought comes into our mind and the more vivid it becomes. Such thoughts can manifest if not checked, particularly the more self-destructive ones - 'where your attention goes your energy flows'. The secret is, of course, to cut off the source of energy in whatever way best suits us. One way is to acknowledge the thought, stop pretending it doesn't exist and face it by asking ourselves what is it we fear? Due to the Law of Equilibrium, a stronger force is needed to overcome the bothersome one. For example, the only way to stop thinking about pink elephants is to constantly remind ourself that there is no such thing. Likewise, to stop thinking about shadows we have to remember that light is the maker of shadows and again keep reminding ourselves that nothing can withstand Light, Love and Truth. Simple prayers to God will also help. Once the thought's source of nourishment (as here, our attention) is cut off, it will start to weaken and will eventually disappear.

The same principle applies for Satanic obsessions. Where Churches or Groups put a great deal of attention into this, distortions and confusions, two fundamental tools of dark forces, will subtly enter in. This applies to the 'teachers' and 'priests' who preach that the only ones who will be 'saved' are those within the Doctrine, and all the rest of us are 'bound by Satan and destined for eternal damnation'. The warning signs are things such as Judgement of others and the desire to control their followers, to the extent they won't take too kindly if their ways are questioned. *Fear* is therefore the key to survival for such Doctrines, not God's love and light.

It is easy for innocent victims to fall prey to such Churches or Groups when they go along 'to find God in their lives'. Initially they may be impressed by the conviction and show of strength by the teacher/priest, particularly at the way he/she 'frees' people from Satan using various rites and rituals. The individual will then become concerned that they themselves may be full of various evil Spirits having never even entertained such a possibility before. The more the person focuses on such things, the more they will attract them resulting in the usual confusion, fear and possibly nightmares. The 'master' will gradually pour more coals on this fire until the individual is so fearful that they become totally dependant upon the Doctrine.

As discussed previously in this Chapter, it is possible to become possessed. However, this can only happen when we give such

Lower Etheric 'demons' or people a way in. By weakening our powerful natural protection via, for example, very heavy drinking, drugs, continuously focusing our thoughts on all the negative aspects of our lives at the expense of anything remotely positive (self-pity), and thinking, sometimes obsessively, about demons, ghouls and so on, and/or dabbling with such things, then we will attract the corresponding energy/entity - Law of Attraction. Hence, the problems always begin with us.

Darkness only exists in this world and the Etheric - getting less and less the higher we rise to the Light. In our darker moments it helps to remember that God is *all powerful* and the sun is always above the clouds no matter how big the storm. Therefore, the more positive we are and the more love we have within and around us and the stronger our Faith becomes, the less chance there is of any Lower Etheric entity being able to creep in. At the end of the day any state other than being ourselves, in alignment with God, without anybody or 'thing' influencing or even controlling us is our objective.

FOOTNOTE: 'The Trial' gives an excellent portrayal of what it is like for those Spirits trapped in the 'Lower Etheric'. Everybody in the book/film is at the same level of Inner Density. For example, the one on trial is arrogant and damning of practically everybody, the others in the courtroom are cruel, crude and get immense pleasure at seeing another apparently worse off than themselves, and the Judge and Jury are not remotely interested in any aspect of the Trial, their sole focus being on Pornographic magazines they have beneath their desk. In the case of the lawyer, who appears interested and helpful at the beginning, it gradually becomes apparent that his overriding desire is the carnal lust he has for his secretary.

Silence and contemplation is the way out, but for those in the corridors awaiting their Trial, a huge change of consciousness is necessary. This is because the Trial itself is irrelevant, being symbolic of wanting others to fight their battles for them and always looking to 'outside' propensities for answers as to why their situation is as it is. Hence, the dominance of all the base emotions of blame, bitterness, confusion and Fear. This is the state of mind that these people were in during their earthly lives, and the Spirit is enveloped in such a dense cloud after so many years thinking this way, that it is no wonder it takes some souls hundreds of years of contemplation to realise that maybe they have been on the wrong track. It is only then that a flicker of light will appear as the individual makes a conscious decision to look within themselves as to why they are in their current, miserable situation. The joy and celebration in Heaven once the Spirit embarks on the road to repentance cannot be underestimated. 'I say unto you, that likewise joy shall be in heaven over one sinner that repenteth, more than over ninety and nine just persons, which need no repentance.' Luke 15 vs 7. The Fear of looking within and discovering some fairly horrific things about ourselves is normally far worse than actually doing it. Humility, honesty and praying for forgiveness are the main means by which such souls in the Lower Etheric lighten their inner density.

The leading character in the Trial is the type who whilst on earth had always had more money and power than the average person and no doubt abused such gifts by, for example, satisfying his sexual fantasies, and exerting his 'superior status' by publicly putting others down at dinner parties, for example. How many people in this day and age due to social and financial factors demonstrate such traits from time to time in some degree. Extreme cases might never be able to climb down from their arrogant pedestal and could remain in such a state of unconsciousness for eternity - in the Lower Etheric and during their incarnations (remember there is no change in psyche at Physical death). Should the 'shocks' discussed in the final Chapter fail to wake them up, then they may end up so entrenched in the density of the Lower Etheric and corresponding physical incarnations that they can't or won't face up to themselves even when the Day of Judgement approaches. In this case, as mentioned, they will end up as one of the 'tares' and meet with Spiritual Death.

As the individual looks within with an honest conscience and heart, he may be appalled by the way he's been and daunted by the Karmic burden he has built up which needs atonement before his Spirit is free. Should he sincerely and humbly pray to God for forgiveness and help in releasing some of his Karma, it is not surprising that the Spirit of the person (independent of whether the mind of the person is aware of their 'path' or not) jumps at the chance of a life of sacrifice and suffering during which time he can work off a proportion of his Karmic baggage and move closer to the light of God. (This is expanded upon in the last two chapters). This desire and 'need' for the light is in the Spirit of everyone of us and is the main purpose of our life on earth. Remember whatever our family/situation, this is ideal for our particular Spiritual Growth and epitomises God's universal love for all mankind. It is also possible, as mentioned, that the Spirit needs this final shock to free their last piece of Karma before they enter Heaven.

15. FAITH AND ITS CONSEQUENCES

Faith means conviction in God. Conviction means 'firm belief', in that we are convinced beyond all doubt of God's existence and supremacy and can therefore put our complete trust in Him, give Him total loyalty, steadfastness and fidelity, and live our lives according to all the ramifications of this. But, the Spiritual Quest begins with 'tentative hope' not faith. Faith comes later and is tried and tested, lost and found, pushed and shoved and stretched to its limits until the end of our days, 'if ye had faith as a grain of mustard seed ....' Luke 17 vs 6. Once we have some measure of real Faith then this can be built upon.

Faith in God is defined perfectly in Hebrews 11 vs 1:- 'Now faith is the substance of things hoped for, the evidence of things not seen.' Hebrews 11 summarises some of the wonderful examples of Faith from the Old Testament, such as that of Noah:- 'By faith Noah, being warned of God of things not seen as yet, moved with fear, prepared an ark to the saving of his house; by the which he condemned the world, and became heir of the righteousness which is by faith.' Hebrews 11 vs 7.

One who truly walks in the way of God will treat every person he meets at the very least on equal terms, if not greater than himself. He will simply wish to give and receive nothing in return and will not be deterred in any way if, in his giving, he is shunned, ridiculed or persecuted. This is because in his deep Faith he has an Inner Knowing that all is as it should be, and whatever lesson/challenge he and his fellow man are getting, it is the best for his and their Spiritual Growth/ development. 'Marvel not, my brethren, if the world hate you. We know that we have passed from death into life, because we love the brethren (everyone). He that loveth not his brother abideth in death.' 1 John 3 vs 13, 14. Until we can have some measure of Faith and stand firm in Truth no matter what is thrown at us with love in our hearts for all mankind, then the light of God will not be able to enter our beings and we will remain dead inside.

One of the things that 'Enlightened ones', who capture the imagination of the populace such as Jesus, John the Baptist and Ghandi etc., have in common, is that *all* suffer persecution of one kind or another and many seem to meet a sticky end. The world, in an overall sense, despises *Truth*, and governments fear those who work things out for themselves and opt for God's Law instead of theirs, where no amount of man's chains can bind them. This will mean suffering whilst on earth:- 'By faith Moses, when he was come to years, refused to be called the son of the Pharaoh's daughter; Choosing rather to suffer affliction with the people of God, than to enjoy the pleasures of sin for a season.' Hebrews 11 vs 24, 25.

Authorities will try anything to prevent others with true conviction from interfering with their rigid doctrine. For example, before Jesus was murdered, they tried everything to blacken his name and ridicule him:- 'This fellow doth not cast out devils, but by Beelzebub the Prince of the Devils,' Matthew 12 vs 24. This was a favourite accusation, but Jesus logically pointed out that the Devil would 'look after his own' rather than cast them out. - 'If Satan cast out Satan he is divided against himself; and how shall then his Kingdom stand.' Matthew 12 vs 26.

Why do people who walk in the light get persecuted we may ask? If a person goes into 'dark' surroundings, such as streets or certain areas and they are literally 'bathed in light', then this will illuminate their surroundings, so that they will see clearly where others may not. But, because they are illuminated, then it is easy for 'everybody else' to see them clearly. When this happens and such a person allows themselves to be totally exposed to others in the light sowing love where there is hatred, then those whose Spirits have a denser cloud about them may react with jealousy, envy and bitterness as they glimpse, consciously or otherwise, their own failings reflected back at them. Such emotions if allowed to continue unchecked (the individual's choice) will result in anger, hatred and hence a further darkening of the person's Spirit. It is in this state that they will blame and vent their anger, due to their own shortcomings, on the 'enlightened one'.

The life of the one who walks in God's light is therefore no picnic, due to the persecution by others and, as is the case for everybody else, they are themselves tempted every day of their lives with the 'appropriate tests'. Should the one in 'the light' fail a challenge in accordance with God's Universal Laws, an increase in Inner Density will be the result as the light of God is dimmed and maybe even switched off. This will then require some hard work on the part of the individual to switch the light back on again:- 'No man having put his hand to the plough, and looking back, is fit for the Kingdom of God.' Luke 9 vs 62.

'He that entereth not by the door into the sheepfold, but climbeth up some other way, the same is a thief and a robber.' John 10 vs 1. *There is no such thing as a short cut to enlightenment* and there is no substitute for *hard work* (contrary to many 'New Age' beliefs). Hence, a good medium, channeller or healer has worked very, very hard on themselves to lighten their Inner Density, so that they can contact the Higher Beings with greater knowledge and thereby glean more valuable information. This is the same as anybody who has worked hard to live according to a high standard of morals and values, in that they receive similar blessings from above, whether they are conscious of this or not. In other words an individual's resistance to the Light is reduced relative to the blockages within that they have worked on easing or clearing altogether.

These days there are many Cults, Sects, New Age and Spiritualist Groups that work on moving closer to 'The Light'. This is good but, should we hear talk of:- 'Now I've (or we've) 'Ascended' into the fifth, seventh or whatever Level of Light Body or Dimension', and we feel more elevated or Spiritual than another (in no matter how small a way), then Lucifer has begun to enter in. In such cases, it doesn't matter how much Unconditional Love we may feel and project; if the *humility* is not there, our *ego* is being tickled, with all the many potential dangers.

'Thou shalt not tempt the Lord thy God.' Matthew 4 vs 7. The same applies should we start performing 'tricks', to show off to ourselves or others, such as turning the TV on and off or changing channels, using only our minds. It is hard enough for an average person to remain humble and keep their feet on the ground, but how much more so for people in the public eye, such as politicians and those worshipped by millions, such as top sportsmen and rock stars. It is a healthy attitude to strive to do the best we can in our chosen profession - this ties in with the Spiritual point of working to the best of our ability in everything we do. However, the other Spiritual values are all of equal importance.

The objective for all of us must be to make ourselves as clear a channel as possible for the Divine Spirit to work through us. This is not possible until we are prepared to look deep into ourselves and our dark sides and do the necessary emotional clearing, by focusing with full awareness on the lessons 'presented to us' in every moment of the day. This will mean a breakdown in our old, rigid beliefs and practices, and a craving to work within the laws of creation with love, expecting no reward from man. 'Take heed that ye do not your alms before men, to be seen of them; otherwise ye have no reward of your father which is in Heaven ...' Matthew 6 vs 1, but with the faith and knowledge that our soul/Spirit Spark from God is recording every action, thought, word and deed on which we shall be *judged*.

'Therefore when thou doest thine alms, do not sound a trumpet before thee, as the hypocrites do in the Synagogues and in the streets, that they may have glory of men. Verily I say unto you, they have their reward.' Matthew 6 vs 2. Would we rather milk the adoration of men for our deeds and achievements *or* have the love of God and lay up our Treasures in Heaven?

'Therefore, whosoever heareth these sayings of mine, *and* doeth them, I will liken him unto a wise man which built his house upon a rock: And the rain descended, and the floods came, and the winds blew, and beat upon that house; and it fell not: for it was founded upon a rock. And the foolish man built his house on the sand which fell and great was the fall of it.' Matthew 7 vs 24 - 27. We will know when we are aligned and carrying out God's Will, because our Faith will be as a rock, and no matter what is thrown at us we will stand firm in Truth, projecting love and humility. If we think 'we've got it', - the Blade of Grass will be blown to show up our weak point, thereby pointing out to us whether our Faith is built on rock or sand.

When we connect with the Divine Energy, as can sometimes happen when we take a 'leap of faith', we stand firm in Truth with love in our hearts and confront an obstacle, person or situation head on and leave the outcome (which is rarely what we imagine) to God's Will. In these situations, when we burst out the other side, we get a feeling of euphoria, joy, clarity, and a surge of energy coursing through our bodies. If the outcome was separation from our partner or job and we have stood firm with love, and received this surge, we know, no matter what, that it has been the best for all parties concerned. However, should we feel confused and drained, our body/mind is telling us that we are receiving the lesson in the wrong way.

Confusion and feeling drained are warnings which, if ignored, can lead to disease and hence greater challenges and shocks to wake us up. Therefore, our health and corresponding lightness of heart are ideal indicators as to our Spiritual Development. This is not to say we are 'bad' if we become ill, but we need to be aware that the illness is telling us something which, if we allow it, could enable us to further our Spiritual growth. It may help to ask, 'what is this illness preventing me from doing?' Then work from there.

When fully awake, we will have no fear of man. If we have deceived ourselves, which is very easy to do, we will still have some degree of fear within us. Remember, Fear is lack of *Faith*. The process of awakening may take many lifetimes or just one, but when it happens a state of such joy, gentleness, love and happiness encompasses us and enables us to give ourselves freely to the world, in the knowledge that we are doing God's work. The inner state of divine love makes all earthly pleasures - drinking, smoking, sex, whatever - seem about as exciting as watching grass grow. Such people will remain in this state even when stuck for five hours in an M5 traffic jam.

Spiritually enlightened people, such as the Dali Lama, not only inspire help through their prayers and what they say, but also through their *actions*. They inspire by meeting the atrocities of the world head on and by *never* displaying any hatred towards those who have inflicted the suffering, because they understand the workings of God's Laws in Creation. 'When you see God you laugh a lot' -The Dali Lama. When he was asked what he hoped to achieve from meeting the world politicians he replied:- 'If I can get them to open up just a little ...' Once we open up our hearts in no matter how small a way, then this gives God a way in. This is similar to the first few molecules of water penetrating the husk of a seed, but whilst we maintain a hard outer coating, we will remain dormant. Such beings as the Dali Lama enter the Spiritual Realm - provided, of course, that they are one hundred per cent pure at the end of this life:- 'Verily I say unto you, among them that are born of women, there hath not risen a greater than John the Baptist: notwithstanding he that is least in the Kingdom of Heaven is greater than he.' Matthew 11 vs 11 - a very tall order indeed!

In the light of the above, if we presume that due to our religious beliefs and dedication, we will definitely go to heaven alongside Christ when we die, with even the minutest implication/feeling that there are others in the world who won't make it, then watch out! This demonstrates a lack of humility and means that we are vain. 'Heaven' is the realm of purity and God decides who is worthy enough to enter - not us, in the same way as it is our Spirit in alignment with His Universal Laws that decides when we are ready for our next lessons on the Spiritual ladder.

'And I, brethren, could not speak unto you as unto spiritual, but as unto carnal, even as unto babes in Christ. I have fed you with milk, and not with meat: for hitherto ye were not able to bear it, neither yet now are ye able.' 1 Corinthians 3 vs 1, 2. Paul humbly states his own limitations, and suggests that any arrogance or vanity will mean that we are still being 'fed with milk', as opposed to the tougher, Spiritually demanding yet more nourishing 'meat'. Hence, any presumptuous thinking could mean we're in for a nasty shock at Death. Also, whilst incarnate, our Faith will always be tested until the day we die, and depending on how we cope we will either Spiritually rise or fall:- 'No man, having put his hand to the plough, and looking back, is fit for the Kingdom of God.' Luke 9 vs 62.

Abraham had one of the ultimate tests of his Faith when God asked him to make a sacrifice of his Son. Even though he knew that killing another was a sin, he was still prepared to do it for God. This has since become one of the most distorted concepts, because more people have killed in the name of God than for any other reason. However, the *significance* here was that once Abraham had proven his Faith in God, God 'stepped' in and stopped him before he committed the deed. (Genesis 22: 1- 13).

'He that loveth father or mother more than me is not worthy of me: and he that loveth son or daughter more than me is not worthy of me.' Matthew 10 vs 37. To what extent do we love and have Faith in God? Are we prepared to stand up against even our own family, and be discarded by them indefinitely, should our family's will be different to God's Will? 'The children of this world marry, and are given in marriage: But they which will be accounted worthy to obtain that world, and the resurrection from the dead neither marry, nor are given in marriage;' Luke 20, vs 34 - 35. Are we really married solely to God, or solely to our fellow man? God looks upon our hearts and cannot be deceived - would we leave our loved ones and material security if this were God's wishes? And, if not, then just how serious are we in our love for God and carrying out His will? And do we really believe that Heaven, the realm of eternal life, peace and light, actually exists? Or do we deep down just feel it's a nice idea, but may be a bit boring compared to what it's like downstairs?

'There is no man that hath left house, or parents, or brethren, or wife, or children, for the Kingdom of God's sake, who shall not receive manifold more in this present time, and in the world to come life everlasting.' Luke 18 vs 29 - 30. The point being, in these cases, is that how do we know we're doing it for the 'Kingdom of God's sake?' The answer, as always, lies in our emotions and how we feel deep down. Should we feel anger, resentment or bitterness, then we feel guilty and are more than likely doing it for selfish reasons. Therefore, each individual needs to resolve all such lessons with a clear conscience and if we can maintain this at all times, particularly when we're being wrongly judged, it means our Faith is strong, we're aligning with God's Will and doing what we do for 'The Kingdom of God's sake'. For example, God commanded us to, 'Honour thy father and mother.' Matthew 15 vs 4. This means having understanding and respect for our family at all times, especially when we're doing the opposite to what they'd like us to be doing.

Blind faith in man is damaging; i.e. just blindly accepting what another tells us, or what we have read. Therefore, there's nothing wrong with being sceptical, questioning everything (especially the contents of this book!) and asking God for help in discriminating and understanding. Blind Faith demonstrates indolence/laziness and a desire to let others fight our battles for us and blame them when things don't work out.

'If the blind lead the blind, both shall fall into the ditch,' Matthew 15 vs 14. It's up to us to find out what's right and wrong and if we blindly follow a false Spiritual Master and/or Doctrine, both will receive Reciprocal Action. However, if our volition is for the good, and we aim to give unconditionally of ourselves and not worry about what we may receive in return, we will be protected in all that we do. Hence, if we do follow a false doctrine, we will come unstuck yet, provided our eyes are open, we will learn an invaluable lesson, such as to 'Only Trust God'.

Faith in its pure and simple truth is summed up in the words of Ghandi:- 'I may say that I have never been interested in a historical Jesus, I should not care if it were proved by someone that the man called Jesus never lived, and that what was written in the Gospels was a figment of the writers imagination, for the Sermon on the Mount would still be true for me.' Or are we like 'Doubting Thomas' who needed to see the holes in Jesus' hands and side:- 'Blessed are they that have not seen, and yet have believed.' John 20 vs 29.

16. THE 'IGNORANT' AND THE 'INTELLECTUAL'

We reap what we sow. A loving, open-minded person could find the whole Truth of Creation and its hidden mysteries by watching, experiencing and simply working with nature. God's Will is one hundred per cent fair, which means that 'His' knowledge is just as available to a tribesman as it is to an intelligent Don. 'I thank thee, O father, Lord of heaven and earth, because thou hast hid these things from the wise and prudent, and hast revealed them unto babes.' Matthew 11 vs 25.

Therefore, the evidence of God's Will is as much in nature as it is in the Bible or other books of Truth. The Parable of the sower: If we plant a seed in poor ground, no matter what we do to it, it will not bear much fruit. Similarly, if we plant a seed in good ground and then don't look after it, it may well become choked by thistles and other weeds, or wilt if the weather becomes too dry. Hence, ideally we should plant our seeds in good ground, and work hard to nurture and care for the plant as it grows.

Many people throughout the world have a passion to keep some sort of garden, be it a window box, or a border/borders, and they derive immense pleasure from it. The 'gardener' will endeavour to help every plant seek to preserve its life, to increase it to full growth, and to unfold to its maximum flowering and fruition. At the same time he will prune away all weeds and try to pull them up roots and all, knowing that even if he carelessly leaves the merest speck of the weeds' roots, then the same weeds will grow back. A simple thing such as caring for plants to help their growth allows the feeling of God's humility, love and nurture to flow through us and filter from our subconscious to our conscious. This then can be reflected in how we live our day to day lives and in how we deal with situations, thereby lightening our Inner Density.

It is Fear and the Earthly Intellectual Dominance that is one of the main consequences of the so called 'Fall of Man'. The intellect has been very heavily relied upon, particularly in modern times, at the expense of our Intuitive Faculty (inner knowing). Tribesmen living in the wild appear, in some cases, to rely on their intuition first, using their intellect to back it up, work things out and then act on a practical level - could this not be the way God wished it from the start? Some successful people do rely quite heavily on their intuition/gut feeling, but on the whole we are conditioned in the Western Education system to regurgitate parrot-fashion from the volumes of books that we're made to read. This often puts us off such books - including the Bible, for the rest of our lives, similar to when we're not allowed to go and play football until we've finished our bowl of stodgy, solidified rice pudding, which normally ends up in our pockets when teacher's not looking, and certainly means we'll avoid rice pudding in the future, given the choice.

It is in trying to get the *balance* between Intuitive and Intellectual development that is vital. This is true in everything. However, due to the large reliance upon our earthly intellect, in a global sense (Law of Equilibrium) our Intuitive Perception is all but snuffed out, misinterpreted or is mis-represented, and hence Fear reigns. With fear comes the base emotions, such as greed, jealousy, pride, anger and selfishness.

Governments today encourage a ruthless business mentality, because the more money we make, the better their Balance of Payments from the taxes we pay, which lengthens their period of *power*. *But we rather than God are responsible*, through our Free Will for creating this situation, and in so doing we have played straight into the hands of Lucifer.

Modern agriculture is rapidly destroying the countryside, wildlife and watercourses:- The easiest way to cope with this and over production would be to put heavy duties on inputs of sprays and fertilisers, and use such revenue to subsidise organic farming, which would result in about eighty per cent of current production. This would mean less unemployment as more people would be needed to work the land (weeding etc.), and major chemical factories would go bankrupt, thereby reducing pollution. But since man in general serves Mammon, not God, we and many government ministers have shares in such chemical companies and this revenue helps keep them in power. This is a simplistic answer to our Agricultural problems due to the very complex economic situation that we have created. However, will this situation ever change without a radical breakdown in the present economic system? 'And this is the condemnation that light is come into the world, and men loved darkness rather than light.' John 3 vs 19. Or in the words of Bob Marley:- 'And it seems like total destruction's the only solution!'

Have we not dug too deep a hole because of our present ways and values, to avoid a global catastrophe, via, for example, pollution or war? And are we capable of making the fundamental changes from our present state of low synergy (Spiritual awareness and ability to work together in every sense), to a state of high synergy, without 'the aid of' a disaster of horrendous magnitude? This would mean that we would *all* need to become fully aware of the strong connection we have with each other, the planet and the universe.

Such a change in consciousness has now become imperative for the continuation of this planet. A common example in our daily lives of this 'low synergy' and the damaging effects is:- If we wake up tired and fed up, we may become unnecessarily aggressive and barge past someone to get the last bus or train seat. This may well put the other person in a filthy mood, whose fuse is then immediately shortened for the rest of the day, so that he takes it out on the wife and children when he gets home with further repercussions and so on ... Like attracts like - the Karma will always return, even if it's just in a further darkening of our surroundings which, of course, directly affects us and all those with whom we come into contact. Sadly, most of us believe that nature is here for us, and that WE are more important than our surroundings. However, has such self-importance got us anywhere, and if it continues, will we have a planet healthy enough to maintain our 'Important State?'

We can all help and partake in this change of consciousness, by being an example to all those with whom we come into contact and by giving and expecting nothing in return - in contrast to how most of us currently live our lives and conduct our business. We also need to shed the attitude of, 'what difference can I make when much of the world is at war and Third World countries are cutting down the rain forests as rapidly as ever'. Every bit of good we do brings some much needed light into the world. The 'why bother' attitude not only signifies our indolence, but is damaging to ourselves. This is because it is in 'giving' to others and our surroundings that we are directly giving to ourselves and furthering our Spiritual Growth.

As in all things, *love* is the key. 'Love thy neighbour as thyself' - but how or why should or can we love an apparent warmonger such as Saddam Hussein for example? Rather than hatred we should sow love, as like it or not, we are all connected. It is possible to have compassion for such a person surrounded by body guards and their conscience, and because of the state of their Spirit shrouded in *fear*. In hating and not forgiving another for anything, we are directly blocking our own Spiritual Growth, as discussed in the chapter on Judgement. As to the likes of Hussein and Hitler, God loves *all* mankind without distinction and wants us all to return to Heaven as a mature Spirit. However, Base desires, actions, words and thoughts of people who commit great wrongs create a very dense cloud about their Spirits, and this is intensified by the similar energies of their followers (Law of Attraction).

To break free from the temptations and emotions concerning the 'things of the earth' and the quagmire of the treacle-like Lower Etheric, can involve such a huge letting go and change of our current personality/character that we are terrified there won't be anything left of us. It is easy to see why some of us shirk from looking within ourselves indefinitely. In these cases, Spiritual Death is our destiny on the Day of Judgement.

'If a man says, I love God, and hateth his brother, he is a liar: for he that loveth not his brother whom he hath seen, how can he love God whom he hath not seen?' 1 John 4 vs 20. If we cannot 'Love our Neighbour', (which includes our enemies) and continue to treat Like with Like - hatred with hatred, aggression with aggression and so on, are we helping our fellow man to make any changes in the way he thinks and acts? Also, if we keep trading an 'eye for an eye', and we are all *connected*, will we ever break this vicious cycle of selfishness, separation and pride that Lucifer so gleefully basks in? We can, of course, only ever do the best we can, and provided we endeavour to maintain a state of Grace and project Love in every situation, we will always be helping ourselves, others and the planet.

'And if the house be worthy, let your peace come upon it: but if it be not worthy, let your peace return to you.' Matthew 10 vs 13. Should our love be persistently hurled back in our face, there is nothing we can do but walk away with love and 'shake off the dust of our feet .' Matthew 10 vs 14. This will prove difficult when it is someone close to us, but should our Grace crack, as it may when we're fighting a losing battle, our Spirit will become contaminated again and we will no longer be able to do God's Work. Also, for all we know, a person may need to go down a certain supposedly 'wrong' path to learn a specific Spiritual lesson - discussed further later.

It is God's wish that everybody should enter a state of Grace/ selfless love with one another - how else can the beauty of this planet be realised? Yet, the Law of Equilibrium suggests that the humble few, who stand in God's Light, have a long, hard and seemingly impossible task ahead - just look at how Christ was reviled and persecuted for simply standing firm in God's Truth. 'If they have persecuted me, they will also persecute you.' John 15 vs 20. The number of people employed in the Military, Police Forces, Law Courts, Solicitors Offices and such like world-wide, is a reflection of how far we've strayed from God Centredness and the extent to which we have the Lucifer energy entrenched in our lives.

'But if ye forgive not men their trespasses, neither will your father forgive your trespasses.' Matthew 6 vs 15. If we *hate*, it is like holding a giant mirror up in front of ourselves, which directly affects and damages our Spirit and corresponding Inner Density. However, we as a race are partly responsible. For example, in our *greed*, we sold Hussein and many others the 'Tools of Destruction', and are now 'Reaping what we've sown', in accordance with God's Will.

This is not to say that it was right or wrong to have attacked

Hussein's forces, but it is certainly a part of our Karma. Likewise, it is necessary to tell off a small child when it has done wrong, and this helps the child to learn and develop with a balanced view of life. The difference between the two is we generally don't give a three year old an AK 47 to do as it pleases for six months, without receiving some major Reciprocal Action.

17. SUFFERING

No Blade of Grass... There is no such thing as a life not worth living, no matter what state we're in -mental or physical. As mentioned, our health and type of illness is something which we have attracted to ourselves and is necessary for our Spirit. Even when fate seems to be taken out of our hands, no matter what we may try to do, it's up to us to face it with the correct attitude - with Humility and Love.

Suffering taken on board in this manner is the greatest possible deed a man can perform with the corresponding Reciprocal Action; 'A blessing in disguise ....' Again we can either rise or fall. Many of us have been guilty of selfishly moaning about a mere cold, when there are those in pain twenty four hours a day from a terminal disease who never once complain, their sole concern being for their loved ones suffering as a result. It is not hard to see how, through suffering, our base emotions of selfishness, anger and impatience, come to the surface and thereby show us our weak spots and hence the area of ourselves on which we need to work. 'The life of man upon earth is a trial.' Job; whilst we are not yet in the Kingdom of Heaven, we must expect suffering.

Job's integrity and Faith in God was tested to the limit. Even though he was a 'good' man in alignment with God's Will, and loyal, caring and generous with all those with whom he came into contact, Satan (the Lucifer energy) was 'allowed' by God to tempt Job's Faith to the limit. As Job was stripped of all his worldly goods, which caused not even a flinch of doubt in God, Satan told God that he (Job) would, 'curse thee to thy face', Job 2 vs 5, as he then 'smote Job with sore boils from the sole of his foot unto his crown'. Job 2 vs 7.

Such extremes of suffering are little more than a huge Karmic lesson to prove our worth to God and move closer to him. Job was tempted to renounce God during his intense suffering and felt very sorry for himself at times, but he stood firm in his heart and humbled himself before God in the end. 'I have heard of thee by the hearing of the ear: but now mine eye seeth thee. Wherefore I abhor myself, and repent in dust and ashes.' Job 42 vs 5, 6. Having suffered and come through his test, Job was then rewarded very handsomely by God:- 'And the Lord turned the captivity of Job, when he prayed for his friends: also the Lord gave Job twice as much as he had before.' Job 42 vs 10.

Once an emotion is released, we normally feel much better as the way is cleared for a calmer, relaxed, even loving state to fill the space left behind. For example, a small child tends to display immediately an emotion pertinent to a situation, such as crying. Once he/she stops crying, the incident is normally finished and/or forgotten, allowing a calmness to fill in behind - unless the child sulks, in which case it has not cried enough and is still suppressing part of the emotion. Likewise, when something happens beyond our control concerning close friends or relations of which we deeply disapprove, our initial response gives us a clear indication as to where *we are* Spiritually and the state of our Faith: Whether we feel deep compassion and love for all concerned, or unequivocal anger and judgmental blame directed at the 'supposed' guilty party.

As mentioned earlier, to be unjustly accused is one of the

greatest tests for the human Spirit. In such circumstances, can we project back love, humility and forgiveness? However, how often do people let their judgements and the judgements of others, harden their hearts, giving rise to family feuds, bitterness and sorrow, which may take years to heal. If there is still no forgiveness and a loved one dies, regret and guilt may fill the void, binding the Spirit still further:- 'Agree with thine adversary quickly ...' Matthew 5 vs 24 - 26.

In today's society we are educated to have to justify our actions to others and various authorities from schools, to councils, some (but not all) religious establishments or gatherings, parents, friends, workmates and all manner of fixed authority. The self-righteousness and the domination of the pampered ego of many politicians, who spend their lives 'passing the buck' and blaming others for the mistakes they've made, is a reflection of the general state/equilibrium we're in. This is because if a politician was brave and humble enough to hold his hand up and apologise when he makes a mistake, then we, the general public, would demand that he resign from his job. Therefore, the current system that we have all created, places little or no emphasis on the Spiritual aspects, but it certainly provides a good 'testing ground!'

When we are 'judged' by others, rightly or wrongly, our emotional response, as discussed, gives us a precise indication as to how we're progressing Spiritually. However, to get to a stage when we are able to put our trust in God over and above anything and anybody, this will often have resulted from building upon intense suffering that we have experienced when we have hit rock bottom at some point in our life. It must be remembered that there is a huge gulf between not being bothered by what others think of us - arrogance, and having sincere compassion, love and understanding, and actively projecting this back to the one who's judging us.

When we hit rock bottom, however that happens, and have nobody to lean on in any way except for God, then we have the ideal opportunity to radically transform and view life differently in accordance with God's Will - if we so choose. This same principle applies to many aspects of life. For example, some heroin addicts need to touch on 'death's door' before they are shocked into having to make a major change in their lives and find the inner strength to give up the drug. Hitting rock bottom, in whatever situation, means that we have no choice but to admit our lives are out of order/control and we are powerless to do anything about it without help - preferably from God through whatever means He chooses. This doesn't always have to be a painful experience, but the pain does tend to be relative to how humble we are and how much love we have in our hearts.

The Prodigal Son, far from home, dirty, lonely and hungry, envying the pigs their swill amid his degradation, is each one of us in our alienated, sinful condition. The prodigal son eventually crept back, totally deflated and humbled, seeking a slave's status. The last thing he expected was a huge celebration, symbolic of the forgiveness of God. But this only happened when he had reached the bottom of the abyss and had nowhere or nobody to turn to except God.

Should we feel depressed and then focus on the reasons why, we will get such answers as 'I've not got a girlfriend or a boyfriend and am never likely to have one; nobody loves me or really cares; and I'm so bored/fed up with my job and or situation'. Our focus of attention is centred to a very large extent on ourselves - personal desires, shortcomings and what we apparently cannot have out of life. We then get very good at justifying to ourselves and others that our lot is worse than anybody else's and 'nobody else could possibly understand what we are going through'. But, what of the crippled African child with no money, who still manages to give a radiant smile? Faith and Hope are extinguished relative to the extent we wallow in such thoughts. However, most significantly, Charity and Love and our ability and desire to Give can be all but eradicated. Being that it's only in 'the giving we receive', our depression will intensify as we become more self-indulgent.

There are examples all around us of people forgiving their adversary no matter what the crime, and those who show concern, compassion and love for others in all circumstances. We often hear comments about such people like, 'they seem to radiate a certain something!' Should therefore a therapist, professional or otherwise, ask a person, 'what are your needs?' or, 'what do you want out of this?' Are they not sometimes encouraging further self-indulgence and selfishness. An exception is if the therapist gains the information to help the individual to think about others, and get them to see the damage their indulgence is doing to themselves.

We may ask about the 'depression' some people feel when working with the mentally handicapped or terminally ill? Such doctors and nurses will sometimes feel daunted and drained by the extent of suffering, particularly those working in war-torn and/or third world countries. They will also feel deep sadness and compassion for those suffering, but because they are 'giving', this is different to depression, because the light remains on inside due to their Faith and belief in their work (unless, of course, they indulge in the attitudes of 'poor me' and self-pity). If Mother Theresa became 'depressed', would she still be able to help the suffering masses in the slums of Calcutta, aged nearly ninety?

Once we realise that God's love is the source of all love and provides us with every comfort we could possibly want, then we will no longer worry about how others feel about us. It will be a surprisingly big weight off our shoulders when we can say to our parents or someone of great influence in our lives, who feel that what we are doing is radically wrong, irresponsible and so on, (but we feel it's right for us,) - 'okay, so we beg to differ. Thank you for your advice, which I respect, but I will make my own decisions.' If we are sincerely projecting back love, we will remain emotionally calm, no matter how much the other disagrees, disapproves and judges us. Also, by pouring no coals on the fire and projecting love, the energy will dissipate. But, if the one judging us senses even the slightest chink outside of love, then they may well persist all the more.

The importance of suffering and how we deal with it can be likened to the ancient myth about a Knight reaching a fast flowing, boulder-ridden river. Here he meets a bossy, selfish, unpleasant old hag, demanding that he carry her across, which due to his good, humble nature, he decides to do (though she certainly doesn't appear to deserve it!). During the crossing, she bellows orders and beats him across the head until he nearly drowns, and so he is naturally tempted to chuck her off a number of times. However, when he does eventually reach the other side utterly exhausted, and puts her down, she turns into a beautiful Princess. This is an illustration of how Love can transform even the darkest things to light, but calm persistence and long-suffering endurance are often the only ways to see things through.

For example, this is frequently the case when trying to put to rights the Karma with another person, when it has become very heavy due to the relationship having become overly entwined, obsessive and with a predominantly mammon or carnal focus. Should we try to strike out at the heart of the dragon (chapter on Fear), we may often get the impression that we are not making any progress at all. Our partner, family member or friend knows us so well that if they don't want to change or the situation to change, they know exactly how to side step, deflect or create an illusion to maintain the status quo. The other party may be miserable at the time, but are so terrified at losing their safety net and discovering some potentially hard hitting Truths about themselves, that they do anything to prevent this situation. We will often feel frustrated, drained and even angry at the apparent futility of all our attempts. However, when the Karma between us and another has built up to such an extent, we will need to strike at the heart of the dragon not once but many times and like the Knight humbly show ourselves and calmly persist in seeking the Truth in often the stickiest of circumstances. This will mean we go down before we start to come up. It is like peeling an onion whereby even though we may attempt to go for the heart each time, we may only get one onion skin per strike which will often feel as though we are getting nowhere. The temptation to give up will, at times, seem overwhelming. However, with long-suffering endurance we will reach the heart and the Karma will be cleared.

18. NO BLADE OF GRASS - SOME EXAMPLES

PEOPLE: - Take the Law of Attraction whereby the Etheric Energy Field (Aura) around our bodies has what could be likened to a number of templates and hooks, allowing others to 'hook in' to our templates and we to theirs - *if* like attracts like. If not compatible, people will not be able to hook into each other's templates -their hooks will just slip off and vice versa. Due to the ever moving, changing universe, this can mean that as people change (and hence their hooks and templates), we can no longer hook into those we 'hooked into' in the past, nor they into us; hence, a change in friends or partners may be one of many results of this phenomenon.

Therefore, for Inner Stability and peace on Earth, *hook not with fervour into the transient - only the eternal.* Divine Intention ensures people or circumstances come into our lives to bring to our attention any imperfections within us. If their hooks hurt and we feel Fear and any of the Base Emotions, we are being shown that there is still more work to be done. In other words we are being 'encouraged' to work on changing the shape of our templates, for example, by working on bringing more light and love into our beings so that these particular hooks no longer affect us negatively:- 'Cleanse first that which is *within* the cup and platter, that the outside of them may be clean also.' Matthew 23 vs 26. This is not to say we can't or shouldn't have relationships, we can have a fantastically beautiful relationship with another. *But*, if we desire to control or possess another in no matter how small a way, and/or put them before God in our hearts, we can expect troubles (as discussed in the Chapter on The Family).

DISEASE:- One of the best ways of understanding diseases is to see them as gifts from God. Disease, like everything else, manifests in accordance with the Four Laws of Creation. For example, if we keep running round the problems given to us, where Emotional Suppression and the corresponding blockages are the result, and if we keep refusing to take note and 'look within' to find the answer, we will make ourselves ill. Needless to say, obstacles and corresponding diseases will increase in intensity if we keep insisting on running away - many good books have been written on this subject. For example, Cancer is said to manifest as a result of some deep seated resentment, bitterness, sorrow or any suppressed emotion, which if not faced up to, can kill us. As far as our Spirit is concerned there is not a lot of point staying on Earth if our Spirit is stagnating and we refuse to look within. Someone who has recovered from serious illness (and there are many who do) is often a much nicer person, more humble and lives for each precious moment. No Blade of Grass ... and that goes for *all 'accidents'* also - as in all things our Spirit has attracted the situation because we, and probably others, need the experience for our/ their growth.

KIDNAPPING: To take the example of child-kidnapping, then before incarnating, the child may have accepted this 'destiny' (see *Footnote later*), receiving the corresponding Reciprocal Action and lightening of Density. For example, this may be to give the Earthly Mother and family one of the ultimate challenges of:- 'Love thine enemy,' and:- 'But if ye forgive not men their trespasses, neither will your father forgive yours.' Matthew 6 vs 14 - Law of Return. The same principle applies when a child dies young, or even if it gets an illness. In the giving of its life for the 'benefit' of another's Spiritual Development, the child will receive the corresponding Karmic benefit for its Spirit. The parents and relations will naturally be hugely affected. They will either become humbled with all the corresponding benefits for their Spiritual growth, or conversely become resentful and bitter - the choice, as always, is ours.

Whatever happens in this life, we should always put our Faith in God. This doesn't mean the 'Blissy', 'oh well it's His Will, so let it be'. God demands action, and thus there is nothing wrong with using all the Tools available - police, detectives and so forth. The test lies in maintaining a state of *grace*. If a tragedy happens, we get the best possible results by keeping calm and level headed and maintaining our focus on God with the Faith and knowledge that whatever is happening in our lives is in accordance with the Four Laws. After all, we can only ever do the best we can.

'Who is my Mother? and who are my brethren? And he stretched forth his hand towards his disciples and said, behold my mother and my brethren! For whosoever shall do the Will off my father which is in Heaven, the same is my brother, and sister and mother.' Matthew 12 vs 48 - 50. Keeping our focus and love upon God above all else, will certainly help keep our emotions in check during times of crisis. As mentioned earlier, if we bring children into this world, it is our absolute responsibility to bring them up in accordance with God's Will, as best we can, *but* always in the knowledge that they are God's children *not ours*: To possess in any way is *not love* and can lead to dangerous emotional distortions at times of minor or major crises in our lives.

FOOTNOTE: The 'destiny' of a person's life pattern is determined by the laws, not by choice, because the laws work automatically. In other words, our pure Spirit spark deep within our being will, in alignment with God's Will, chooses the incarnation which will give us the best opportunities for our Spirit to mature. This will normally conflict with our current 'personal' desires.

ABUSE, VIOLATION AND MOLESTATION:- To take the above principles one stage further to the sensitive issues of Rape and any type of molestation and violation, sexual or otherwise - No Blade of Grass ... Every experience is relative to the vulnerability and strength of the individual. For example, the consequences for an old lady who has her handbag stolen in the street may be the same as for somebody who is raped. Likewise, to some women the violation incurred from being raped may be so great they may feel that they might as well have been murdered.

'And as Jesus passed by, he saw a man which was blind from his birth. And his disciples asked him, saying, Master, who did sin, this man, or his parents, that he was born blind? Jesus answered, Neither has this man sinned, nor his parents: but that the works of God should be made manifest in him.' John 9 vs 1 - 3. The child or family member who is kidnapped, abused, raped, murdered, born disabled, deaf, dumb, blind and so on, will reap some very positive Reciprocal action for making the 'sacrifice' and giving their family the lessons they need for their Spiritual Growth. Whether this is working off an old Karmic debt of their own and/or simply reaping positive Reciprocal action for allowing themselves to be used by God for the benefit of others, is between their Spirit and God. With regard to a young child dying of starvation and disease in the shanty towns of Third World Countries, the consequences have a huge effect on close family and the village. They should also have a similar effect on their 'neighbours' throughout the world, showing all of us there's something very wrong with the way we do our business, run our countries, and our attitudes and priorities-all of which we need to change if we are to live according to how God would like us to live. The Karmic consequences for the Spirit of the one making such a 'sacrifice', to give us the opportunity to change the way we live our lives, are colossal. Also a child which dies at two years old is unlikely to build up any new Karma. This means that they are far more likely to fulfil their life's purpose than those of us who live a much longer life and are faced with succumbing to temptations every day of our lives.

In cases more familiar in Western society, we may again ask how appalling tragedies can be of benefit to those who love and care for the victim? To take an example of parents who give birth to a child badly disabled in some way: Before the child is born, assume that the mother and father are the types who quarrel over the pettiest of things, entrenched in the familiar base emotions of jealousy, envy, anger and so on - all of which amounts to a power struggle for 'supremacy' in the relationship, whereby the two constantly battle to possess and control the other. Once one party 'gets on top' he or she feels a gleeful satisfaction in dominating the other, with a feeling of 'this proves I was right all along'. The other half ends up inwardly dead, stifled and submissive. The idea of standing up for themselves about anything against their dominant, self-righteous partner is too exhausting to even contemplate, and even too frightening - domestic violence being common place in such situations. The 'Universe' for the two parties is, of course, very small, confined and dense, and this may have been the case for many hundreds, even thousands of years as the two Spirits moved between the Lower Etheric and similar incarnations where they were given the 'opportunities' to break free from their shackles - but didn't or wouldn't.

Should then the couple give birth to a disabled child, this will radically shake up their environment and, 'short of getting rid of the child', they will be forced into making a change. The seeds of compassion and caring for another, so deeply buried in a cloud in the past, may well start to grow and blossom as they not only look after their child but also their partner. Should this compassion be sustained then this will be the 'entry point' for God's love, resulting in the corresponding lightening of the individual's inner density. The focus on the child will generally mean the petty disagreements and arguments of the past will markedly reduce.

However, it doesn't have to work this way, because the couple are only given the 'opportunity to grow' and owing to Free Will, one or both of them can choose to run away from such responsibilities and therefore themselves, with the corresponding effect on their Inner Density. 'Let brotherly love continue. Be not forgetful to entertain strangers: for thereby some have entertained angels unawares.' Hebrews 13 vs 1 and 2. Is it not very possible that an Angel can come into our lives in a wheelchair?

The same principles apply to all shocks we have in life - our Spirit in accordance with God's Will, has attracted these challenges for our growth. Should our child be violated in any way or even murdered what would be the effect on the parents? Taking the example of the couple mentioned above, they might well be seething with hatred and vengeance directed towards the offender. However, the opportunity is there to have compassion for their partner as they share the hurt together, provided they are not totally submerged in hatred and self-pity. Once this seed of compassion is activated then, as mentioned, this can be the entry point for God's love to enter.

This sounds a very drastic method of awakening, but it cannot be stressed enough that our Spirit may very well have tried everything else over the past hundreds of years to get us to change and begin the climb out of the quagmire we have created for ourselves. Such drastic action will be very much a last resort but, as we many of us know, our pride and stubbornness can be very, very entrenched. Even though we may be filled with hatred for the perpetrator, we may well have never felt compassion before for anyone, so at least this is a start. It could well prove a very long climb up towards God's light, because eventually we will have to forgive the offender - discussed in the Footnote at the end.

What if such a shock should happen in the family of a happily married couple who love each other and help others? Naturally, the compassion and love for each other will flow freely and easily in this situation, as they support one another. Hence, their Spirits have more than likely attracted this test to give them the ultimate challenge in forgiveness - the importance of not judging the specifics of another's situation are again apparent. As mentioned earlier, we need to be one hundred per cent pure before God allows us into True Heaven and we have 'out' of this Karmic cycle once and for all. We are down on earth to change and grow, which is why our Spirit in accordance with God's Laws will not allow us to stagnate for too long. Also, it is important to stress again that due to our Free Will, we have created our surroundings, *not God*, and we have only got ourselves to blame that our Spirits have to attract such radical wake up calls - 'big tests' are now common place throughout the world.

To take rape as an example, there is a theory that the raped in this life was the rapist in a past life. However, according to the Law of Gravitation, if the rapist in a previous life was caught and suffered for the rest of his life in jail, he would have worked off some of his Karma relative to his inner suffering from guilt and the degree of his repentance. The remaining Karma will need to be worked off in his next life/lives, through perhaps different lessons/experiences, but 'whatever you sow that you will reap', maybe he'll get Aids the next time round? If it's not like this, how could the cycle of rapist/raped be broken? In such a situation, the present day legal system of jailing the rapist is performing an act of love and doing that individual's Spirit a favour, even if he only works off some of his Karma. This is provided he shows remorse and sincere regret. If he remains unrepentant, the returning Karma may be so great that the rapist feels incapable of looking at themselves and atoning for his sins. Should he remain bound in this state come the Day of Judgement he will meet with Spiritual Death.

One thing which is for sure is that the offender will receive the full Karma/Reciprocal Action for allowing Lucifer to take control. We all have a Spirit Spark within us and know when we are doing right or wrong, and have the freedom of choice to listen or keep our fingers in our ears. The weaker the person, the easier for Lucifer to enter in. However, he always acts as a 'tool' in accordance with God's Laws and sometimes even Divine Intention. For example, Judas Iscariot, being the weakest of the Disciples was used by the Lucifer energy to betray Jesus and fulfil the prophesy:- 'The son of man goeth as it is written, but woe unto that man by whom the Son of Man is betrayed! It had been good for that man if he had not been born.' Matthew 26 vs 24. The returning Karma for such a deed meant that Judas' Inner Density at death was worse off than when he was born. There are theories that the likes of Judas and rapists in carrying out their deeds and making a 'sacrifice' of themselves in providing another with a 'lesson', thereby giving them the opportunity to shed more of their Karmic debt, in some way get rewarded. However, such theories would make a mockery of Jesus' word and God's Will, and hence is impossible. *We* reap whatever *we* sow.

What of the *raped person* who has undergone one of the ultimate tests in humiliation, degradation and violation? As mentioned, God Himself does not inflict anything upon us; it is through the Universal Law of Cause and Effect and our free choice that we have created our current environment. Hence, either the 'victim' has made a 'sacrifice' of themselves so that, 'the works of God should be made manifest in them', with the corresponding reciprocal action, or else it is to help them work off a Karmic debt sown sometime in their past. Even if we believe in coincidences and that things happen at random, there is still no denying the Karmic consequences/repercussions resulting from such circumstances. Hence, Rape and violation is always Karmically related for both the violator and the victim. In such cases, the victim has one of the ultimate opportunities to grow. Again, do our priorities lie with Mammon and our earthly pleasures or our Spiritual Growth? 'And fear not them which kill the body, but are not able to kill the soul; but rather fear him which is able to destroy both soul and body in hell.' Matthew 10 vs 28. The lighter our Inner Density, the more we will understand this concept. Should we bear a high level of Spiritual awareness and are seriously violated, this may be our last Karmic challenge in, for example, forgiveness, as mentioned. The more God centred we are the easier this will be - the value of an inner knowledge of the Laws of the Universe are very apparent.

It must never be construed that the raped 'deserves' what they get. We can none of us know whether somewhere down the line a 'seed was sown' or not. The Karmic 'needs' of another is strictly personal between the individual and their Spirit working in alignment with the Four Laws. Hence, it is impossible for anybody else to pinpoint the plight of another with any accuracy, and in saying that someone 'deserves' what they're getting will automatically result in a build up of karma of similar energies for the one making the Judgement - law of Attraction. We may well ask what seed could we have possibly sown to warrant such horrendous violation? There are, of course, numerous speculative possibilities, such as the individual may have been a rapist or torturer in a past life, but whatever, that's between the individual's Spirit and God.

Love, humility and *forgiveness* is the key to all things and the key to maximum Spiritual Progress. Hence, if the raped person can genuinely and sincerely forgive the rapist, this marks the end of the Karma involved for the 'raped'. This applies to any victim of any kind of assault or injustice - major or minor.

Should the victim believe some or all of the Karma of the rapist is alleviated when she forgives him - and it bothers her, then she has not sincerely forgiven. Forgiving another is the ultimate act of compassion and love, and in so doing raises the individual's Spirit to the next level for their next set of tests. The aggressor will still reap what they have sown - remember Judas Iscariot. *See Footnote on Forgiveness.*

There are, of course, degrees of rape and violation. In the most extreme cases, some people may never be able to have sex again and simply can't forgive? Such people may suffer for the rest of their lives and through such suffering will release more of their Karmic burden. However, being that there is no change in psyche at death the individual will carry their emotions over with them. Whether they 'let go' of their bitterness, hurt or anger in the Etheric or in future lives is entirely down to them, but let go they must if they are to be totally free from that particular Karmic cycle.

It has been mentioned repeatedly that we are all connected. As a result of this the raped receives further good Karma due to the effect this has on her family and close friends, because in the shaking of their foundations, they are given the opportunity (albeit to a lesser extent than the victim) to further develop Spiritually - should they so choose! If we truly accept the Spiritual Life, we will know that nothing happens by chance, but for those who are earth or materially orientated, then everything does appear to be governed by the throw of a dice. No Blade of Grass... takes into account everything, everybody and every situation - not just the Reciprocal Action resulting from idle gossip and coincidental meetings.

However, a note of encouragement lies in the definition of Karma, whereby - 'sincerely exerting ourselves to the good, we can greatly modify the nature and result of the returning Karmic Repercussions.' For example, if our Karmic burden merits release by rape then by our earnest efforts in striving towards the Light, we can alter the same reciprocal action to perhaps just having our private diary discovered and exposed by another. This is a reflection of God's love for mankind.

FOOTNOTE: FORGIVENESS. Sincere forgiveness on the part of any victim is the one hundred per cent desire to free the perpetrator of all the Karma they have built up through their deed - wicked or otherwise. We all reap whatever we sow, but if the perpetrator genuinely acknowledges their wrong doing to themselves, God and the victim and fully comes to terms with the shame and evil within them, *and* then makes the corresponding changes in their persona, so that they will never inflict such suffering on another again: This is *repentance* and will mark the end of the Karma - provided they are also fully forgiven by their victim (see below). Christ when 'healing', in whatever sense or circumstance, first forgave them their sins and emphasised the importance of Faith:- 'Thy Faith hath made thee whole.' Matthew 9 vs 22, then told them to 'Go and sin no more'.

However, if there is a trace of pride, stubbornness, ego or resentment in their repentance, then not only will the Karma remain, but the individual will build up more Karma, by holding on to such Base Emotions. Also, if the victim does not forgive, then not only does he/she bind themselves with this emotion for as long as it takes to release it, but also no matter how much the perpetrator repents, they will never be totally *free* from their deed until the victim has completely let go and is free from the experience themselves. It must be stressed again that we are all connected Karmically with each other and the Universe. 'Forgive us our debts, as we forgive our debtors.' Matthew 6 vs 12. 'Then came Peter to him, and said, Lord, how oft shall my brother sin against me, and I forgive him? till seven times? Jesus saith unto him, I say not unto thee, until seven times: but, until seventy times seven.' Matthew 18 vs 21, 22. *Forgiveness is the key to our salvation.*

Once it is recognised that without God, nothing has any point or meaning, a greater acceptance of all that life on earth is about can be achieved. This 'acceptance' means that we willingly open our arms to life with all our hopes set upon God. Though it is sad that the wicked prolong their days and the righteous are trodden down, we will still look to God - not to plead with him to destroy the wicked or avenge the good, but with *faithful* acceptance of current affairs, knowing that at the right time God will deal Justice. In these situations with our understanding at a certain level of maturity, we will pray that strength be given to the weak, the ill, oppressed and so forth. Likewise, that mercy and forgiveness be given to the wicked because, when the time comes for God to judge the earth, any who are standing on the wrong side of the line will be facing a Judge that knows all things, sees all things and reveals all things. It will not go well with them, so pray therefore that this happens to no one, no matter how evil or dark they are on earth. *Forgive* these people for all their wrongs, sins or crimes and pray that they may be delivered from their own evil.

GHOULISH 'SYMPATHISERS':- The knock-on effect and Reciprocal Action from any disaster can be colossal, not only for the neighbours and relatives, but also because of modern communication (newspapers and television) which enables millions to hear about it and be affected by it. (See Footnote). There are many genuine compassionate sympathisers, but there are also the Ghoulish types with a Crisis mentality who often talk of little else. The more energy they put into such thinking, the harder they may find it to conceal their excitement as news of yet another earthquake or murder comes in. Such people will stand in a crowd nodding their heads at a dreadful road accident, but with a slight glint in their eye at someone else being worse off than themselves.

If they are isolated in some way, and shaken from their crisis reverie, they will tend to panic as a sheep does when it's picked out in a flock:- 'How could this be happening to me when there's so many more to choose from?' 'As a man thinketh in his heart, so is he.' Proverbs 23 vs 7. If we can't control our thoughts, the emotions and the body will also not be controlled, because action or manifestation follows thought. This can stimulate further thought, which if not controlled will lead to further action or manifestation. A vicious circle indeed when spiralling downwards. Due to the Law of Attraction, such people tend to hear of disasters before anyone else, but the Inner Density of *all* those who hear is affected, depending on their response: Whether this be compassion for all concerned, or compassion for the victim and hatred for the offender, or pleasure at the thought that there are yet more people 'who're worse off than me', or just simple indifference. Our Spirit attracts everything into our lives - even the things we hear about - No Blade of Grass..., to give us the opportunities to grow, should we so choose; so in the words of Jeremy Beadle:- 'Watch out, next time it could be you!'

FOOTNOTE: The mediums of film, television, newspapers and books are very powerful and should never be underestimated. Violent, pornographic and/or frightening films have a far greater influence on us than we realise - and not just on our conscious mind. The ninety per cent of our brain that we apparently 'don't use' - our subconscious, also absorbs and records the images, which is why our dreams are often influenced in some degree by our recent 'viewing'. Children noticeably have more nightmares if they have seen something frightening on television.

We many of us are not strong enough to erase many of the images from our minds for some time, and there's no knowing how much our subconscious has absorbed. Unfortunately here Like attracts Like, and the more we 'enjoy' violent, pornographic films and so on, the more our thoughts become centred upon such things. Therefore, the more films of a certain kind that we see the more energy we give to such thoughts and the greater the chance of manifestation in our lives. For example, there are many cases of violence in our streets similar to the type of film being shown in the local cinema at the time. Watching a 'sexy' film can stir up our carnal lust and eventually result in sexual abuse of another, a passionate affair behind our wife's or partner's back, or simply in more lustful glances at bathing beauties and/or other people in the street. 'But I say unto you, that whosoever looketh on a woman to lust after her hath committed adultery with her already in his heart.' Matthew 5 vs 28. Such a focus *definitely* erases the light of God from our beings.

A case study, demonstrating purely 'Karmic' principles, on mass murder triggered by influences such as a violent film or films, media coverage and such like.

The Karma for the perpetrator of such a deed has been discussed fully in the previous section on Molestation. The exact same principles apply whatever our deed. However, the Karmic consequences can be very far reaching and potentially damaging for many of us. Should somebody embark on a maniacal killing spree using his own guns, for which he may or may not have a licence, and triggered by a film that he has just seen, then all of our Karmic loads could be affected in a number of ways.

In an ideal world ('Heaven' on Earth - Path A) there would be no guns or violence. Should we be a gun owner, we are in effect directly supporting an industry which is responsible for making a product that has been and will be used to take the lives of others. Likewise, with violent films which often glamorise violence with handsome, heroic actors playing the trigger happy 'baddy' - or 'goody' (violence is after all violence from whatever angle). Should we enjoy watching such films (whether it be we pay to go into a cinema or simply watch them on TV), not even necessarily the exact film that was responsible for giving an unbalanced person the idea for mass murder, then again we are supporting an industry which directly triggers the loss of human life. We are therefore partially responsible. Karma builds up not just from the effects such films have on our thoughts, subconscious and actions, but if enough of us didn't own guns and watch violent films, then such industries wouldn't have the financial support to survive. The fact that we many of us 'support' one or both of the above industries could well mean we continue to add more baggage to our Karmic load.

It must also be remembered that energy generated cannot be destroyed (until such time as it is redeemed or fulfilled, when it simply changes). Therefore, the more we get a thrill from violent/whatever scenes, then the more we give energy/power to certain 'Like' entities in the Lower Etheric (due to the Law of Attraction) which happily feed off our thoughts/energies. These entities can then further fuel and encourage another who is even more imbalanced than ourselves, in addition to giving yet more energy to the thoughts that we have resulting from the films we watch. The more coals we pour onto our particular fire, the harder it becomes for us to break free from our addiction. As mentioned, energy in the form of thoughts will eventually result in manifestation, resulting in more thoughts and so on. Whether manifestation comes from us or another of a 'like mind', the effect on our own Inner Density needs no explanation.

What of the men, women and children mown down in the crossfire? The fact that there are no coincidences means that the Spirit of each individual knows and understands what is happening and there is a very good reason for it - Karmically speaking. For example, the individuals may be making the ultimate sacrifice by giving up the current 'cloak' that they are wearing to show a nation and even the world how far removed we are from the way God would have us live our lives, similar to some African children who die of starvation aged two. For this the Karmic benefits again need no explanation.

Law of Equilibrium - the problem is globally speaking, we

have the Lucifer energy so entrenched in our lives that even though we may ask most of the right questions in newspapers and on television after a tragedy happens, such as 'what about the absurd gun laws and violence on the screen?' we never really do anything about it. This is primarily due to our love of Mammon over and above all things Spiritual - the *cost* to any government of banning violent, pornographic etc., films in the cinema and on television makes any real change currently impossible to see. Also the outcry from a nation if their 'favourite films' were banned would probably be enough to force a government out of office!

We can argue endlessly about stronger censorship and maybe draw the line at Cowboy and Indian films. However, even these films have a degree of influence, particularly on children who like to mimic screen heroes such as Custer. 'Heaven on Earth' means no violence and guns, so is it too great a sacrifice to forgo films depicting any form of violence, if this means even just one fellow human is saved from a terrifying, bloodthirsty Death? It is estimated that an American child has on average seen 1,500 murders on the screen by the time he/she is fourteen.

Likewise, if guns were universally banned. Again due to the *cost*, cleaning up the streets and houses of guns would not be contemplated at present. There would also be a need to disband guns in the police force and the army, due to the resultant thriving black market.

The only way forward is for all of us, in every country, to voluntarily lay down and destroy our weapons, having learnt from the many violent tragedies, wars and so on. Sadly, these increasingly frequent tragedies seem to make us more blinkered, producing more weapons and attitudes of vengeance, revenge and mistrust. *But*, this is our choice. 'For all they that take the sword shall perish with the sword.' Matthew 26 vs 52.

The main thing that we are shown from the sacrifice made by victims in a terrible tragedy is the need to start by changing our own lives. Not only do we not have to watch violent films, we don't need to own a gun - our Faith in God and His Will being the only protection we need and that really works anyway. However, if we chance on violent scenes on TV, which is almost impossible not to these days, the more light and love of God we have in our hearts, the more disgusting and upsetting we will find the predominantly lower Etheric focus of such TV and cinema. It is then we are more likely to do the ideal, due to the Law of Attraction - switch the telly off! The trouble is, as mentioned, that images have just as great an effect on those of us who are apparently less 'sensitive', who then actively turn the TV on when there's a promise of violence, pornography and/or horror.

Such Tragedies should also make us ask ourselves questions such as, 'to what extent do we love our neighbour as ourself?' Our 'neighbour' also includes the misfits and apparent 'weirdos' in society, who no doubt need even more love than what we give to those closest to us. How often do we avoid, shun and mentally sweep under the carpet a certain individual in our neighbourhood we really don't much care for and feel uneasy about. 'For if there come unto your assembly a man with a gold ring, in goodly apparel, and there come in also a poor man in vile raiment; And ye have respect to him that weareth the gay clothing, and say unto him, Sit thou here in a good place; and say to the poor, Stand thou there, or sit here under my footstool: Are ye not then partial in yourselves, and are become judges of evil thoughts?' James 2 vs 2 - 4.

Loving thy neighbour as ourself, means treating everybody at the very least as an equal (humility) and giving such people the time of day, a welcoming smile, talking to them and allowing them to talk to us with no condemnation. Should we 'judge' them in any way they will avoid us from thereon. Talking is one of the most powerful healing mediums of all - we all of us feel much better once we have got something off our chests. Who knows what the loners in society build up in their minds and bottle up, with nobody to listen to them and show them any love? As the pressure in the bottle reaches a certain point with the release valve firmly shut and kept shut by the neighbours, there comes a point, due to the laws of physics, when it will explode. Should the loner then kill a load of innocent victims, then not only can we get rid of our gun, if we have one, and withdraw our support from films which fuel and often glamorise violence, but focus on our love for our neighbour. Who knows, by humbly giving our time to the 'local weirdo', we may help to inadvertently avert a tragedy in the future.

Overall, we are a very long way from truly loving our neighbour as ourselves. This means that tragedies will continue until we all make some radical changes in the way we live our lives. Sadly we are not very good at learning from our mistakes. We only have to look at what we have learnt from two world wars this century with the loss of millions of lives, yet there are now more tools of destruction in the world than at any time in History. If Hitler had been brought up in a community of unconditional love, where everybody loved their neighbour the same as themselves, mother or wife, with no talk of aggression, war and so on, then who knows...?

The stronger our Faith becomes, the less we will fear and the more we will realise the extent of the very strong connections between ourselves and our fellow man. 'Loving' our neighbour also means forgiving them their faults and mistakes for all the reasons discussed previously. This means forgiving another for the most horrendous deeds even if we just hear about them but are not directly involved ourselves. The 'I hope they rot in hell' type attitude, is Karmically damaging for us and only helps to keep the world bound in the claws of Darkness.

Flippant forgiveness can be equally damaging. For example, forgiving so as to seem pious, Holy and Christian before others and God, without having sincerely looked into the full implications of the deed for ourselves and others. Gaining as full an understanding as possible about the incident in our hearts, the pain it has caused others and emotions it's given rise to within ourselves, is vital for sincere forgiveness. This done, we then at least must make the necessary changes in our own character and attitudes and try to do the best we can in the future.

Many people blame God for 'letting such an evil deed happen, with His Blessing according to some biblical texts'. This has been a major cause of many good Christians losing their Faith. Firstly, we must remember that God gave man the loving, precious gift of Free Will, and if He 'stepped in' to prevent an 'evil' act of horrendous magnitude, then where would He stop. We all of us sin every day and if God steps in each time, then we would be stripped of our Free Will and end up living in a world of automata. Secondly, such shocks are our *wake up calls*, as discussed above, to show us the extent we and society need to change to even just start aligning with God.

The exact same principles apply regarding the consequences of pornography and lust. Society on the whole encourages, glamorises and even idolises those with an apparently abnormally high sex-drive - even the relatively passive James Bond films have this as a major focus. Such conditioning can make it very very difficult for us to allow the pure energy of God's love to flow through us towards another and ourselves. For example, regarding advertising, even the most obscure, practical, seemingly non-sexually related products are often plugged using sexual innuendos as the main selling point. This says a lot for where most of us are coming from - Law of Equilibrium. Likewise, on going into some of the larger newsagents, we are often hit with racks of fashionable magazines with a gorgeous 'supermodel' pouting at us from the cover and suggestively undoing the third button down on a skimpy blouse. The women and men who currently feature in most adverts, films, magazines and even the popular 'romantic novels' are well above averagely pretty/handsome and very 'sexy'.

The problem is that the more we focus our attention on such stuff the more hang-ups we get. Not only do we become more aware of our own physical failings, but focus more on the physical shortcomings of our partner. Hence, the plastic surgery industry is one of the fastest growing in the world. Many of us find it very hard to detach our attention from such carnal ideals, which keep us bound in darkness and prevent the true essence of God from flowing into and through us.

Due to the universal Law of Attraction, we will keep attracting partners of a similar Inner Density to ourselves with the same hang-ups, obsessions and so on. As in all things this is purely God's design to help us. When we see the problems and falsities in another (which is always easier than seeing them in ourselves), and we open up our hearts to the fact that we are seeing a reflection of the faults within ourselves, then we are provided with the ideal opportunity to make some fundamental changes. The time this takes and extent to which we open our hearts is, of course, down to the individual.

However, there are those who become so overwhelmed by what they read about and see, that their hang-ups gravitate further into massive inferiority complexes to the extent they sexually abuse another. As is the case for violent films and guns, the more we support and are influenced by the 'carnal' industries, the more we ourselves are partially responsible.

Even though the greater mass overcomes the lesser (Law of Equilibrium), the power of the light is the only source of real power. As a small candle flame can light up a dark room, so an equivalent flame of darkness in a light room makes no impression at all. There are plenty of examples throughout history of a small speck of light overcoming an apparently much larger mass of darkness, such as the stories of David and Goliath, and Samson. The one thing such characters have in common is their total Trust and Faith in God. Also, when Abraham asked God whether he would destroy Sodom and Gomorrah if there were fifty righteous people in it, working his way down to ten. '...Peradventure ten shall be found there. And He said, I will not destroy it for ten's sake.' Genesis 18 vs 32. God would not destroy something if there is the smallest pocket of true goodness present. For the above reasons, the attitude of 'there's not a lot of point changing my ways and making sacrifices if very few others are doing likewise', is not only indolent but wholly untrue. Every step we make closer to the light has huge repercussions.

19. CONCLUSION:

The root meaning of the word 'Religion' from Latin means *to unite*. Therefore, why do we continue to judge and kill in God's name? The purpose of religion is to teach people to align solely to God and His Will, which means letting go of all earthly attachments, including the expectations we have for ourselves and others. Attachments to Mammon and expectations give rise to Fear and Judgement, with all the negative connotations, hence, 'to what extent do we allow others their process?'

Allowing others their process means loving them unconditionally i.e. being a safe space for them in all circumstances. Should we have the attitude of, 'I don't think you should do that because I love you', or 'I only want the best for you, which is why I want you to do this', and 'I need you because I love you', or 'I'm only jealous because I love you' and so on, then this is not love. In such situations, we are simply striving to get our personal needs met by clutching and grabbing at another with the desire to manipulate and control them. The '.... because I really love you' line is a frequently used and often effective way, consciously or not, of enslaving another, by making them feel guilty if they don't oblige. The more chains we put around another to enslave and control them, the more we enslave ourselves through such 'obsessions' - Law of Attraction. This is shown to us via the dominance of our own base emotions in these situations. When we are obsessed about someone and attempt to manipulate and control them, then we want them to be different to what they actually are. However, if we are the one being pushed, then as in all such situations, we tend to react against it.

God does not rush our Spiritual progress, so what right do we have to rush the progress of another, and anyway the freer we are the more freedom we give to others, in which case the more rapidly we will all progress. What happens when we see a 'loved one' making a mistake? We have all of us made many mistakes, but approached with our eyes open, then on reflection we will always have learnt a valuable lesson. Hence, making mistakes is our *sacred right*. If we wade into someone's path, we (a) could be depriving them of a lesson they need, (b) cause more hurt and pain as their fears multiply seeing no obvious way out, and (c) drive a wedge between them and us and make it harder for them, once they've made the mistake, to come and talk to us - pride and worry of the 'I told you so!' factor possibly getting in the way. Should somebody ask us, then they are ready to hear what we have to say and we are free to express our opinions - though still, of course, allowing them to make their own decisions. Therefore, the 'I wanted to save them from that because I love them', has a hollow ring to it.

However, should we choose to express our opinions when we see somebody close to us we believe to be making a mistake, we must be prepared to take full responsibility and be aware of all the potential consequences. This is because we are making a judgement. Hence, we need to ask ourselves a few questions before saying something, such as: Is our sole objective to help the other person with genuine love? Is there a trace of condemnation and/or emotional blackmail because we desire them to act or deal with a situation in a certain way? Are we prepared to allow them to make their own decision, whatever that may be, with our blessing, particularly when it doesn't tie in with the 'advice we've given to them?' And, are we prepared to hold our hand up and apologise if in the final outcome our judgement was wrong; whereby they stuck with their original volition which proved to be the best thing for them? If we can answer all these questions positively, then we have not judged/condemned the other party.

In Far Eastern films, books and doctrines, there are many examples of Gurus taking a 'seeker' to the edge of his/her own mind or to the fork in their path, from which there may be a number of options. The Guru then leaves the querent at this point to work out and 'feel' which path is the right one. The decision the individual makes, should they decide to make one, is then their responsibility alone. This is all that any of us can do to help another and indeed is exactly what 'God' does for us, by creating the circumstances to give us the 'opportunities' we need for our Growth. As discussed, if God held our hand and guided us down the correct fork, then we wouldn't be tested at all, therefore there would be no benefit to our Spiritual development and there would be no point in our having Free Will. Also, we can none of us presume to know the reasons behind another's challenges, and what we many of us fail to realise is that there is no such thing as taking the 'wrong path'. This is because should we stray from the path of 'righteousness', we will learn a fairly hefty lesson, provided we wake up to why things are happening as they are. Then when we get back onto our path we will be stronger and better equipped to face our next set of options.

The worst thing that we can do is to remain sitting on the fence/remain on the edge of the precipice. If we avoid making any *decisions* indefinitely, then we will remain lukewarm, stagnant and will not progress Spiritually. This naturally defeats the purpose of our being alive. 'I know thy works, that thou art neither hot nor cold: I would thou wert cold or hot. So then because thou art lukewarm, and neither cold nor hot, I will spue thee out of my mouth. Because thou sayest, I am rich and increased with goods, and have need of nothing: and knowest not that thou art wretched, and miserable, and poor, and blind, and naked. I counsel thee to buy me of gold tried in the fire, that thou mayest be rich.' Revelations 3 vs 15 - 18. In today's society we are educated and encouraged to live as safely as possible, work out all the possibilities when taking a risk and preferably not take one, but rather maintain the 'lukewarm' conventions and traditions of today and always be able to 'justify' ourselves should we make any decisions. However, we can't get any help from the universe when we remain in this 'lukewarm state', taking no risks, and consequently our Spirit becomes stifled - which hurts.

Therefore, other people are like the perfect mirrors for us (and we for them), reflecting, via our emotions, the precise things we need to look at and deal with in ourselves. The same applies to the situation we are in, whether it be watching telly to going on holiday. There is no such thing as a holiday as far as our Spirit is concerned, due to all the wonderful 'opportunities for growth' that are presented to us, such as our plane being delayed, Germans bagging the sunbeds, the extent we complain or not about filthy foreign food and so on. When we can allow our eyes to open, we will see this operating in every moment of our lives and will then humbly thank the person who exposes the dense aspects of ourselves to us.

Due to the Law of Attraction, we will keep attracting similar people and situations indefinitely until we can wake up and project back love. To many of us this 'appears' not to be easy, particularly when it is 'obvious to all and sundry' that we are wholly justified in reacting as we do. When somebody is being hostile and/or underhand, we may feel it is 'impossible' for us to love in such a situation, and anyway the person 'deserves to be taught a damn good lesson, which will help them for the future'. Should we feel like this, then this is fine, God has eternal patience and love, and will allow us to incarnate again and again and so on in a similar situation until we learn our particular lesson. By fighting hatred with hatred, an eye for an eye, then all we are doing is fuelling that energy and helping to create more of the same. Once we can learn to perceive others in a different way, see the light behind the mask and become aware of the 'message' they bring us, it is only then that we will become truly lighter within ourselves and be of far greater service to our surroundings, the planet and God.

It is, therefore, impossible for any human to know exactly what is best for another. If we are not prepared to question ourselves, then we could very well end up by adding more baggage to our already heavy Karmic load. 'Judge not, that ye be not judged. For with what judgement ye judge, ye shall be judged: and with what measure ye mete, it shall be measured to you again.' Matthew 7 vs 1, 2. It is no good judging others unless we ourselves are prepared to be judged. Christ, being the incarnate of God's love, only judged so as to help everybody, particularly the Pharisees, to align with God and understand His Will. Christ judged others as discussed, however, he had more than cleared the 'beam and mote' from his own eye.

However, with regards to the bringing up of children, we, as parents or guardians, are in many ways like 'God' to them. We are the centre of their universe in the early stages of life - the judge, jury and provider of all their daily needs. This puts a tremendous responsibility on our shoulders to bring them up as best we can in alignment with God's Will. For example, by encouraging the child to develop a set of moral values, and teaching them right from wrong. By being a loving, approachable 'safe space', with whom the child respects and has no fear to talk to about anything, especially when they have made a mistake, then we can truly help the child to learn its early lessons and 'get on the right track'. Naturally, a balance is necessary to give them enough rope to learn their individual lessons and not so much that they run riot! Each child is, of course, an individual with individual needs, which each parent must work out for themselves.

A man falls in love with a beautiful butterfly which gently flutters happily around his head and even alights on him from time to time. He 'loves it so much' that he can't bare the thought of the butterfly playing with other butterflies and even leaving him for another man more attractive than he. Such thoughts cause a tightening of his chest and a sickening feeling in the pit of his stomach. He decides that something must be done, so he catches the butterfly in a butterfly net in which he decides to keep it. To begin with he feels a huge weight off his shoulders as the threat of the butterfly leaving him has gone.

However, after a while the butterfly stops fluttering in the net and simply lies down, not even responding to the man's prodding. At the same time the stunning, strikingly beautiful colours of the butterfly's wings were becoming duller, to the extent the man felt the first seeds of doubt surfacing in his mind as to whether he really 'loved' the butterfly after all. Once he could see a vicious circle developing as his 'love' was dwindling relative to the butterfly fading, he decided that he had no choice but to let it go - he also didn't fancy the responsibility and guilt should the butterfly die whilst with him in its current state.

Pretty soon the butterfly was flying around again and regaining its colours. The butterfly didn't leave the man but seldom alighted on him as it had before, and when it did, it took the precaution of landing out of reach of the man, such as on the middle of his back. The man felt all the emotions of 'love' flooding his being again - how could he have ever doubted his 'love' even when the butterfly was ill in his net? At the same time, he found himself becoming frustrated and hurt that the butterfly didn't land on him how it had done before. He also felt uncontrollable jealously welling up inside him as the butterfly spent more of its time playing with other butterflies. He became desperate to have more contact and closeness with the butterfly and would gently reach out to touch it, at the same time as making all the right gestures and facial expressions to encourage a closer bond between them. However, to his frustration the butterfly simply side-stepped his advances.

Eventually his patience ran out and he became angry, concluding that the butterfly was mocking him. Hence, one day he shot out his hand and tore it out the sky, but when he opened his hand he saw that he had broken the butterfly's wings and antennae, so that it could no longer fly or feel. Utterly destroyed he placed the butterfly on a leaf only to see it fall off and crawl into the undergrowth.

Being afraid to let people go in case we lose them will result in the other desiring to tear themselves Free, even if they don't actually do it. Should we 'love' someone and allow them total freedom to walk their path, it is only then that the relationship will truly blossom and grow. 'Love suffereth long, and is kind: love envieth not: love vaunteth not itself, is not puffed up; Doth not behave itself unseemly, seeketh not her own, is not easily provoked, thinketh no evil.' 1 Corinthians 13 vs 4, 5. Love does not bargain, or have expectations of how things are 'supposed to be'. 'No man hath seen God at any time. If we love one another, God dwelleth in us, and his love is perfected in us.' 1 John 4 vs 12. It really is as simple as this.

We most of us find it very difficult to give our partner

unconditional Freedom all the time, even when we do know that this is the only state in which love will continue to blossom, expand and deepen. However, even though we may be the type who understands this Universal Truth and have always consciously given our partner enough line and more, then should we have a weak point/chink, however small, in our conviction, a situation will be 'created' which exposes this to us. For example, when we are feeling down and our self-worth is low and we have a 'chink', we may be tempted to rein our partner in for a short while until we're feeling strong again. We may justify this to ourselves having always 'given them total Freedom, so now they can put themselves out for us a little bit - they owe us more than we owe them anyway'. Such thinking will mean a reversal in the energy of love and a deterioration in the relationship unless firmly checked.

Lucifer will be rubbing his hands and heap first kindling and then coals onto this spark. For example, we may get to rather enjoy flicking our fingers and have our partner pandering to our needs, then gradually forget this was only going to be a temporary period. Our partner may then try to pull away back to how the relationship was, and if we block their desire for Freedom and Trust (love), they may become resentful and even bitter. We may then actively use and express the fact that we've 'always allowed them to do as they pleased, and given to them far more than they've given to us - it's not asking much for a little back ...' Again the degree of selfishness of our partner is not for us to judge and the more selfish we become, with all the corresponding base emotions, then the more love, which is *selfless*, will be choked and expelled from our hearts.

We, of course, have some earthly needs to meet. However, until we learn, understand and embody the universal law of 'it is only in the giving that we receive' and have some measure of Faith and Trust that God will provide that which we need, then we will remain entrenched in this cycle of greed and seeking to fulfil our personal desires. This is the 'I need it, I want it and they shouldn't have it' mentality concerning love, power and money. 'Therefore take no thought, saying, What shall we eat? or, what shall we drink? or, wherewithal shall we be clothed? (For after all these things do the Gentiles seek:) for your heavenly Father knoweth that ye have need of all these things. But seek ye first the Kingdom of God, and his righteousness: and all these things shall be added unto you.' Matthew 6 vs 31 - 33.

A teacher has a student who is forever flitting from one relationship to the next and often thinking about somebody else when he is with his current partner - 'the grass is greener on the other side of the fence' principle. The teacher takes the student down to the seaside and gives the student a bucket with a cord wrapped around the handle and asks the student to fill the bucket. This the student duly does, only to find all the water pouring out of a lot of little holes in the side of the bucket, which he hadn't noticed. This naturally happens every time the student fills up the bucket. Frustrated he hands the bucket back to the master and states that the bucket is more of a sieve than a bucket, and therefore it could never remain full. The master then takes the cord off the bucket and swings it around his head a few times, then hurls it as far as he can out to sea and tells the student, 'now your bucket will always be full'.

The only way we will ever find true, eternal happiness, is when we love God over and above anybody or anything on earth. It is only then that our cup/bucket will fill up and remain full. Christ stresses this when asked by the Pharisees, 'which is the greatest commandment in the Law?' And he said:- 'Thou shalt love the Lord thy God with all thy heart, and with all thy

244

soul, and with all thy mind. This is the first and great commandment. And the second is like unto it, Thou shalt love thy neighbour as thyself.' Matthew 22 vs 37-39. To encompass God and His Will in our hearts above all else takes more hard work by each of us individually than anything we can achieve in an earthly sense.

We frequently get tested on our Love for the Eternal over and above our Love for the transient/earthly. Such challenges often cause us the most pain and may result in an aggressive reaction against God as the density around our Spirit intensifies. 'Think not that I am come to send peace on earth: I come not to send peace, but a sword. For I am come to set a man at variance against his father, and the daughter against her mother, and the daughter in law against her mother in law. And a man's foes shall be they of his own household. He that loveth father or mother more than me is not worthy of me: and he that loveth son or daughter more than me is not worthy of me.' Matthew 10 vs 34 - 37. The 'sword' here is the sword of Truth. This sword forces us to ask ourselves whether we love God over and above our own family and when the answer is 'no', it can often make us very aggressive and possessive - increasing our need to control as opposed to love and let go.

Once we can keep the light within burning brighter than any carnal desires, even when we meet a person with whom we fall 'passionately in love', then we will find lasting happiness in the relationship. If our partner then leaves us we will not be daunted, because our deeper love for God will always ensure this. When we truly have the light of God in our hearts, we will never end up a lonely old man or woman.

God's love for us is so total, forgiving, unending and unconditional it's remarkable. When we fully realise this we will always feel safe but it will also dawn on us that this is how

God would have us love our fellow man - friends *and* 'enemies' alike, turning the other cheek and so on whilst standing firm in Our Truth. If our truth is not God's Truth and we think it is, yet we *humbly* keep our eyes/awareness open, we will soon be shown that we're not on the path of Truth. For example, a Karmic situation will be 'created' which throws up any number of base emotions. As mentioned, making a mistake is our sacred right, and any state outside of Humility and unconditional love shows us there's further changes we need to make within ourselves.

The more we become centred in every moment of the day, and align with our Spirit, the more we are 'guided' in all we say and do. But, the 'dissolution of our pampered Ego-Self' in the process will be very painful, however, the corresponding ecstasy at the completion of each stage makes it totally worthwhile. Hence, the nearer we get to 'Enlightenment', the more we project love to all and sundry, and the more detached we will become emotionally and mentally from all things that are not as God would desire of us. A true Spiritual Master of himself bears a state of Grace and Serenity about him at all times. We too *can* bring the 'Kingdom of Heaven' into our hearts.

The 'challenges' we get are in many ways the same, because the only way to deal with them to grow is with humility and love - unconditional. Hence, all challenges are simply tougher grades/levels of difficulty of the same thing, to prove our Trust and our Love for God over and above all earthly temptations.

The idea is to feel whole, complete and happy living in the present moment and stop fighting, not by force of will, but organically, through understanding our daily lessons and, if possible, a gradual training in Spiritual practices, such as in expanding our awareness/consciousness. This is to help us cultivate a new way of relating to life in which we let go of the fear of facing our battles. When we can do this, we will see life afresh. We will see how each of us creates conflict, see our constant likes and dislikes, and our own prejudice, greed and territoriality. All this is hard for us to look at, but it is most definitely there. Underneath these on-going battles we will see pervasive feelings of incompleteness and fear, which simply keep our heart closed.

When we really open our hearts to things as they are, then we come to rest in the present. Truth is our objective in life and whatever Spiritual practice we choose to follow or use. It is only here and now that we can find the love that we seek - Love in the past is simply memory, and love in the future is fantasy. Only in the reality of the present can we love, awaken, find peace and understanding and true connection with ourselves and the world. The majority of us have spent our lives caught up in expectations and ambitions for the future, and in guilt, regrets, bitterness and/or shame about the past, which takes up most of our energy. As we come into the present, we feel a calmness return and a boost in our energy levels, *but* we also encounter whatever we have been avoiding. This involves all that moves us most deeply - our pain, desires, loss, secret hopes, feelings of loneliness, unworthiness, boredom and unfulfilled expectations, all of which we must courageously deal with if we are to remain in the present.

Therefore, to remain alive in the present demands an ongoing, unwavering commitment. We are all of us on a Spiritual path, which requires us to stop the war not once but many times. Whilst on earth we will constantly be tested and tempted, as mentioned, giving rise to thoughts and reactions which, if not checked, will take us away from the present. When we stop and listen to our body and our feelings, we can feel how each thing we crave or fear propels us out of our hearts into a false idea of how we would like life to be. All our daily lessons are designed to show us the Devil within us at the 'grade'/level appropriate for us, which we can then deal with and replace with God's light and love. This, of course, is our Free choice. 'There is nothing from without a man, that entering into him can defile him : but the things which come out of him, those are they that defile the man. If any man have ears to hear, let him hear.' Mark 7 vs 15, 16.

When we truly let go of things we've always been attached to in our lives, it leaves a void in our consciousness. For example, the thoughts and objects of our imagination which we have become used to falling back on and been our stabilising factor when things have not worked as we would have liked, are no longer relevant. Therefore, our safety net which prevents us from falling into the seemingly bottomless pit of emptiness is gone. This can initially be very frightening as our pattern of familiarity is turned upside down, and we struggle to even find something to just think about.

If we sincerely turn to God during such times, we will feel his light and love stronger than ever. Our minds and hearts will expand into a more universal Truth as we become free from the old attachments which kept us in bondage and our eyes fixed down on our daily troubles at the expense of compassion for the colossal suffering our neighbours are undergoing throughout the globe. It is only when our focus on the latter overrides and dominates our focus on ourselves, that we can be truly a servant of God, with all the corresponding Reciprocal action. When this is present in our lives we will know it and will be well on the way to the giving up of 'self'. In many ways, life is a massive deprogramming of the 'success orientated' education system we currently have in the West, if we are to align with God. The point of Christ going into the wilderness was to remove his 'safety net' once and for all and have nothing to fall back on - except God. This done the pure energy of compassionate love could flow freely through him.

Most of us have met in at least one other person an availability, an open hospitality of mind and heart which knows how to create a friendly space for anyone who comes, especially for the stranger, the frightened or suffering, the wounded or insecure. Such an attitude of compassionate openness grows from deep humility, from a genuine poverty of spirit and personal emptiness. 'Blessed are the meek: for they shall inherit the earth.' Matthew 5 vs 5. If we lack this 'inner poverty' we cannot create a friendly space for everyone; we will tend to be selective because we are mentally dismissing those from whom we do not think we have anything to learn. Or we may be subtly using others because we want to feel, and to be thought, kind and compassionate. In either case the other person will not have room to be himself or herself.

Christ was the embodiment of compassionate love. However, in order to be able to say, 'Come unto me, all ye that Labour and are heavy laden ...', Matthew 11 vs 28-30, and allow his invitation to be accepted, he had to be meek and humble, lowly and poor in heart, or they would have been overwhelmed by him, and not have trusted him and found peace and joy in their souls. But, Christ's *earthly* poverty and emptiness *was* Christ's richness and connection to the light of God.

We are often frightened of helping and giving to others unconditionally due to the 'scarcity factor', whereby there's only 'so much to go around and if I give too much then my family will go without'. Unfortunately, should we have this attitude, we will treat love the same, which is why we refrain from giving 'too much love' to certain people, so we have enough to give to our partner and/or family, and become possessive, paranoid and jealous (in however small a way), when they have close friendships with another outside of our immediate 'circle'.

Love *is* the energy of the Universe and is inexhaustible, hence the more we give the more we will receive and the happier, lighter and more energised we will become. Fighting against it in any way, is exhausting, draining and ultimately damaging to our Spiritual Growth. Therefore, there is a need for most of us to make a monumental change in how we live our lives and react to situations. When we can truly forgive ourselves and others, give of ourselves, and humbly admit our faults *when we see them reflected in another*, we will be amazed at the *change*. Should the other be projecting a negative, hostile energy and we confront them with *love*, then the energy will quickly dissipate because it has nothing to feed off. This is how we truly help another, and it is only when we can project back love in every situation that we Free ourselves from such tests. We can all try this in our daily lives and we will see how it works (provided we stick with it and give it a chance!) - the proof is in the pudding and putting it to the test.

We all have access to God's Truth and His Universal Laws, provided we humbly and sincerely strive for it and are prepared to discover some fairly shocking faults within our characters and make up, particularly concerning our more rigid beliefs and understandings. However, provided we are strong enough to show the humility, and make the necessary changes within and not be like the seed scattered on stony ground, 'And when the sun was up, they were scorched; and because they had no root, they withered away,' or thorny ground; 'and the thorns sprung up, and choked them.' Matthew 13 vs 6, 7, then we will move closer to God.

A question that is frequently asked is, 'are we not demonstrating greater Faith in God and greater humility by worshipping him when we don't know or understand how he operates or why things happen as they do?' For a start, anyone who suggests that they are more humble than another for whatever reason, means that it is the other way around or they have still got a very long way to go before they are humble. Humility is humility from whatever angle we try to approach it. However, the more knowledge we have of the Universe and God's fundamental laws, the more we will become aware of our own limitations - which will always be a *humbling* experience, and the clearer we will see the mistakes we have made and are making and then be able to do something about it. This same principle applies in our daily lives, whereby the more experiences we have and mistakes we make, then provided we learn from them the better we will cope with life's daily hassles. Therefore, as we 'progress' the problems that seemed like mountains in the past become more like mole hills. As mentioned, it is then that we get new bigger challenges/mountains to climb so as to assist our further growth. Such tests would have been 'insurmountable' had we been confronted with them in a less mature state, when we would have been comparatively 'ignorant'.

Also, the more 'knowledge' we have and the more 'light' we embrace in our hearts, the better we can be used by God to carry out 'His Work' and be in active service to others and our surroundings. It is only through such 'giving' of ourselves that we can attain true inner peace, however, the more we embody God's love in our hearts the greater our responsibility:-'No man having put his hand to the plough, and looking back, is fit for the Kingdom of God.' Luke 9 vs 62. For example, if two people commit exactly the same crime and one is ignorant of God's ways and the other has some measure of understanding of God's laws and has 'put his hand to the plough', the returning Karma is far far greater for the latter.

In knowing that there is a definite reason as to why things are happening as they are, then it becomes easier to deal with our challenges more objectively. There is only ever one correct solution to any problem, and that's by tackling the 'heart of the dragon' (Chapter on Fear). Therefore, the less ignorant we are of how things work, the straighter and narrower our path will become, and consequently the more rapidly we will progress Spiritually. This is because it will no longer be necessary to zig zag, sometimes apparently uncontrollably, on all sorts of various tangents to learn what are often some pretty harsh lessons, before progressing on to the next rung of the Spiritual Ladder.

With each step our understanding and hence Faith naturally intensifies. 'But seek ye first the Kingdom of God and his righteousness: and all these things shall be added unto you.' Matthew 6 vs 33. The more we 'know' how God wants us to interact with others and our surroundings, the more we will earnestly and joyously strive to live our lives accordingly. Our fears will correspondingly diminish as we stop worrying about our future in the knowing that God is with us in every second of our day, and the lessons we are receiving are in perfect alignment with His Will. 'There is no fear in love; but perfect love casteth out fear: because fear hath torment. He that feareth is not made perfect in love.' 1 John 4 vs 18.

We all of us have experienced 'Spiritual happenings' in our lives. For example, the many apparent 'what a small world' coincidences, dreams and deep intuitive 'gut feelings', warning us of something or someone, or simply 'telling us something we need to know'. We are educated by many religious and cultural aspects of today's society to turn our backs on such things and even to fear them. Naturally, it is vital not to become obsessed with the unseen, and if we do we may become vulnerable to some of the many pitfalls, as discussed in the Chapter on Lucifer. However, when will we wake up to the fact that we are all a Spirit wearing our appropriate cloaks and *we never die*? Our inner voice, dreams and so on are as 'real' as going to work and are there to help us learn our daily lessons. All we really need to do is to assimilate the information and decide whether to act upon it or not - our free choice. However, it is still important to thank God for it, as we should do for every experience we have in life - good or 'apparently bad'.

The more of us who can align with the energy of God's Universe, instead of fighting against it, the quicker we can raise the consciousness of the planet onto the higher more energised vibration of Love. The consequences will be indefinably beautiful as we all give and help one another. For example, the families in Third World countries will no longer have the need to breed huge families so as to safeguard against starvation during old age, because the whole world will see their 'neighbours' in whichever part of the globe in the same light as their own family, in which case no help will be too much trouble. Hence, Christ's message: 'Who is my mother? and who are my brethren? And he stretched forth his hand towards his disciples, and said Behold my mother and my brethren. For whosoever shall do the will of my father which is in heaven, the same is my brother and sister and mother.' Matthew 12 vs 48 - 50, and 'Love thy neighbour as thyself,' can now be seen in its true and fullest context.

Because we will not be immersed in our daily battles with legal firms, authorities, our conscience and even our time-consuming thoughts of bitterness, envy, superiority or inferiority and so on, we will have the time and energy to love (in the true sense of the word) and help others and the planet.

Such a global redirection of our energies will have colossal repercussions. The more of us who can wake up in alignment with God's Love and break free from the 'scarcity factor' fear, and the pampered ego which fuels such feelings as, 'he loves me more than you', then the quicker the planet will change.

Once we start asking questions such as, 'How can I best be of use to God?' and 'what can I give?' and do things for others and for future generations, then there will no longer be a *reason* for hunger, crying, disease and suffering on earth. Even the 'apparently corrupt' Governments in existence today will get swept along in this Tidal Wave of Love - whether they like it or not, because love conquers all!

God is all loving and wants us all to go to heaven in a matured Spiritual State, and being omnipresent, is in everything and every Being the same. There is no distinction between the holiest man and the worst criminal, *but* the circumstances, and hence tests vary according to the individual's needs. Everything is designed to help us move towards the light.

God's demands for the world as a whole are summed up in Isaiah 45 vs 22 and 23:- 'Look unto me and be ye saved, all the ends of the earth: for I am God and there is none else. I have sworn by myself, the word is gone out of my mouth in righteousness, and shall not return, That unto me every knee shall bow, every tongue shall swear.' - One God, One Love; hence *God's Love, Severity, Justice and Truth are one and the same*.

'No Blade of Grass is blown without Divine Intention,' including this ....

CAN YOU NETWORK AND DISTRIBUTE THIS BOOK?

This book has been self-published. If you would like some copies for your friends or anybody else and you buy five or more copies, there will be 10% discount - postage and packaging free. If you have a bookshop, then normal trade discounts apply - postage and packaging free, contact address shown below. Should you wish for just one or two books, please send a stamp addressed envelope (or enclose an extra 90p per book) with your cheque and the form below. Thank you.

Please clip or photocopy the from below and send your order to:

Hector Christie
Tapeley Park
Instow
North Devon
EX39 4NT

Please send me .... copy(ies) of No Blade Of Grass...
I enclose a cheque for £........... made payable to Hector Christie
Name...
Address...
....
....
....County.................................
Postcode.....................Telephone Number.........................

PLEASE USE BLOCK CAPITALS. If you are writing from overseas, please could you enclose a stamped addressed envelope.